north by north/west

north by north/west

(an attention to frequency)

Chris Campanioni

West Virginia University Press
Morgantown

Library of Congress Cataloging-in-Publication Data
Names: Campanioni, Chris, author.
Title: North by north/west : (an attention to frequency) /
    Chris Campanioni.
Description: First edition. | Morgantown : West Virginia University
    Press, 2025.
Identifiers: LCCN 2024038412 | ISBN 9781959000433 (paperback)
    | ISBN 9781959000440 (ebook)
Subjects: LCGFT: Creative nonfiction.
Classification: LCC PS3603.A4589 N67 2025 | DDC 818/.607
    —dc23/eng/20241217
LC record available at https://lccn.loc.gov/2024038412

For EU safety/GPSR concerns, please direct inquiries to WVUPress@mail.wvu.edu or our physical mailing address at West Virginia University Press / PO Box 6295 / West Virginia University / Morgantown, WV, 26508, USA.

Book and cover design by Than Saffel / WVU Press
Cover image by Chris Campanioni

It seems to me then as if all the moments of our life occupy the
   same space, as if future
events already existed and were only waiting for us to find our way
   to them at last . . .

—W. G. Sebald, *Austerlitz*
(translated by Anthea Bell)

VHS (translator's note)

I remember the first time I saw a VHS, how enamored I was with the black brick, not for what it was but for what it wasn't. What it offered or seemed to offer (even then, as a child—but I couldn't have understood any of this as a child . . . and perhaps that's the point, or one of them: to love without understanding) was an escape from the familiar and singular, where I could press *play*, and catch bits of other stories, other people's lives, other universes merging with the one I was born into, the one I belonged to (if I belonged anywhere), without having to do anything but look, to keep looking, a kind of looking I was more accustomed to do with my eyes shut: to overlay fantasy and imagination on the A/V signal. I liked the slips and interruptions, chance falters in the footage that seemed rhythmic, bodily. My life and the lives of those I knew intimately and the lives of people I would never know— people playing other people, people playing music on a stage, people fucking on command, bodies in a ring, arms locked, swollen flesh against swollen flesh . . . the camera pans to the crowd of other faces, swollen, too, in their own way, and beyond identification—were taped and then taped over, rerecorded until the cassette became a scrapbook of moving images, ritual occasions threaded by marionette bodies (melted, blown out, and then lit again), the fuzzy realism of a handheld gaze as it wanders to the periphery of the frame, implying the promise, but only the promise, of physical contact: not the effect of the camera so much as the hand that holds it up. The joy was not to watch but in watching, to surrender to the thrill of an experience that is a combination and a combination that changes with each viewing. Discrepancy between when the mouth moves and what the mouth breathes out, like a voice grafted, or an image inserted over my heaving expiration (a curiosity for texture; the collaboration of limbs) when the world moves in more than one time signature, when the desire for coincidence betrays any assumption of unity. And as I rewind, as I slide the object into this machine, as it is received, gladly, with a quick, cool suck (a sonic memory I can also feel), I listen for the guts to churn, I listen for the reprocessing of so many originals, so many copies. Can't a book, too, be a VHS? Can I make a book of scraps to replace the text proper (the *proper text*)? A book broker wants me to write more "conventional essays"—I don't like scare quotes, but I want to make sure I am getting this right; getting this wrong. The writer, who can't be trusted, wants to write more cassettes, where each page becomes a strip of magnetic tape that readers can control. What I am doing, or trying to do, or think that I am doing, is working as a collection agent, as someone who collects, except the debt I am after is my own. It takes patience, to assemble the scraps, to wait for the moment when A and B become indistinguishable, reversible, when an original is degraded, when it becomes worth something less and something more. I sometimes have the nerve to think I've waited my whole life for this.

Order of Events

I was born unfinished

I was born unfinished. Sometimes I like to imagine that I was born facing the east, the river a mirage of endless blue and slate gray from my window seat inside an incubator on a hospital floor reserved for other newborns like me. I was born, too, facing the north, but also the west, since, although my father came from Oriente, the eastern tip of Cuba, and my mother arrived here from a small village in northeastern Poland—a village so small it does not appear on most maps—I was the first of us to be born in this country, to which I do and do not nevertheless belong. And because I was born unfinished, a part of me believed that, years later, at a moment so near to us, when my body began to break down, I understood that it was neither incidental nor extraordinary circumstances brought on by acute disease or chronic illness, environmental conditions or ritual habits, but the facts or fault of an origin, of being born two months and two days early, a birthmark or defect that has followed me around, I so soon convinced myself, ever since. I felt that what was hidden inside of me—everything I had carried within myself—was beginning to leak out toward the surface-skin, like a glitch in the source code, which teaches the user about the system at the moment that it induces disruption. So that when I began to lose control of my fingers, when my muscles began to palpitate involuntarily under the flesh, as if my body parts desired, all at once, to engineer a different trajectory for the life of their host, and when my eyes, too, began to stop working together, so that single objects began to split into duplicates, I knew enough, as a maker of objects and images, that all of this had already been written. But maybe that's also exactly why, this business of writing and of being written, that anything done to us can be undone, or rather, adapted, with enough strain and duration, with enough desire to imagine something beyond what appears to be out of our control.

This comes later.

And before—before the sick and shattered body, and the spare moments of acceptance; under a stream of warm water, with emergent steam and a suction-cupped mirror as my only audience, repeat after me: *to accept my condition, and the knowledge of what will happen to me and when*—there was the music of words, which was also their mystery. There is my dad, switching from Spanish to English, as he turns to me and lifts my body into the air so I am almost at the same height as my abuela, to tell me what it is she has asked about her grandson—¿le gustan los cuentos de hadas?—she wants to know if you like fairy tales. Here is my mom placing the speaker between us, so we can both hear the joyful chant of *Sto lat, sto lat*—may you live one hundred years, one hundred years—that heralds every birthday. I often wondered about the village where my family—her cousins and aunts and uncles—lived; what was it like there, and did the air smell different than the air here, since the distance between us could feel like a desert if I counted out each unfamiliar pulse on the other end, but for the common moments of static when a voice emerged, granules compressed and decompressed according to the bandwidth required to make the international connection, and I knew all the same we were connected by more than wires and cables; I understood that I was part of the two places I had had to learn by heart, imagining not just the family I had not yet met and would never meet, but also the rooms in which they sat and spoke, and yet I was there—wasn't I?—every day.

I was, before I learned to speak, surrounded by language, by languages. Spanish, Polish, and English traversed our home at any given moment, and it was because of my lack of fluency—an absence that permitted my fascination: unable to seize the words that swirled around me, I found a refuge from expertise and ownership—that I became a writer. Like many of us, for whom deficiency could serve the gradual thickening of relation, my benediction was my inability, as a child, to know all the words all the way, to know them as if they came from me—forgetting, of course, how everything that comes from us first comes into us, how inside of us are parts of ourselves we cannot understand, much less pronounce. How the logic of multilingualism became a channel for multimedia, and how multimedia became another opening—in my writing and my teaching—to ask questions about the borders placed on literacy, discourse, genre and mode, authorship and address, to say nothing of language itself. To ask questions, too, of the text, asking my students as I'd once asked myself whether one shouldn't only think of themselves as a writer but as a DJ and an architect, and a videographer and a barber and a sous chef and a masseuse and a tailor, too; whether we should not examine creative practices and methods of production in isolation but account for how our writing and reading draw from sensory modalities that are not always privileged or legible within the departmentalization of knowledge, and perhaps more specifically, the offices of communication; whether it wouldn't be best, after all, if we thought of writing as an occasion to think, and not the other way around. Where am I in the stories I read, or watch, or listen to? We begin here as a matter of inquiry but also affinity, if only to disidentify with work that we may feel bears no relation to our material realities, cultural forms, and bodily experiences. I begin here with my students and ask them to allow themselves the daily prayer of writing to know and knowledge as a form of becoming, to write their lives and lived histories into the narratives that have ignored or altered us, to write themselves in as an exercise of, if not fluency, then flow and variation and exchange.

I was born unfinished, but maybe that's the point. To resist completion is to say there is more work to be done. To acknowledge omission is to save this space for all the others. The peopleless beach massaged by the wind and in looking, I felt something. East or west—when I am this far south, at the very edge of the city, where one could have arrived by skating down Ocean until they hit the actual sea, my orientation folds—the air is soup, gelatinous with the knowledge that she will soon bear rain. Behind the network of wires and rails: hovering plastics adrift on the periphery, where each hatch slides open with erratic precision; and behind that, the swelling roughness I'll nurture belatedly, as image. My sequence veers, molecular or chemical, the near-sound of skin's prickling. Here's the mind coming to awareness again after the body wrecked with fever. Here's the sun coming in, rising against the roof of another housing development and its scattered terraces, each floating platform facing the roar of the trains as they prepare to terminate. Here's the glove's beaten leather pushing the damp hair from my eyes, the vapor of sweat hardening onto unclothed flesh, if the hand knows best when passing through systems that conceive of it as one data set in a sack of organs. What is an author but an emissary for transfer. What is a book but the vellum of skin and sensation. The convalescing body, to whom I belong, and its failures, to which I pledge my fidelity. I kept looking, despite diminished visibility, the gust on my cheeks, snow checkering the sand now with momentary pearls, so soon did they disappear that I had the impression of watching my own breath melt into the earth, if the present could be confused for the fugitive past. How do I describe the quality of my mother's voice, for instance, if she were the one reading this (the one writing this), instead of me?

< sequence 1

I prefer writing this out, because I like the sound a memory makes. And every stroke is like being splashed, being held or hooked by unseen arms—click, click. Not the sound of a camera. Closer to the way my eyes operate when I've been looking at you without thinking about looking at you. This is the goal, or would be the goal, if ever there were one. To forget you're there. Or: to forget I've been looking. I can't tell if it's important or unimportant to know which, or to require the choice.

Alighting upon a bite, just now, on the smooth part of my arm, the inside if the outside is what's facing you. This lets me know I'm still wanted. And also: even in solitude, I have guests.

[proposal:] to make everything equally important and equally unimportant

[picture:] a continuous interface in which everything intersects

Wanting—not a thing or experience but another person. To be someone other than myself.

For example, my favorite scene in *North by Northwest* is the one Hitchcock never filmed.

In another notebook, which is open on the table, I've written: I want to know what's the difference between an intended future and an unintended future the things I mean to say or do and the miracle of catachresis.

"How Will I Know," I recited in the mirror, a moment ago, an hour, raising my eyebrows, nodding to myself or at myself, was meant for Janet Jackson. After Jackson's management passed on the song, it went to Whitney Houston, for her eponymous debut studio album, which was released a few months before I was born.

Whenever I try to get the whole picture it buffers, like snow falling outside a stranger's window. There are tableaux I'll never behold, people I'll never encounter, words I'll never taste. Languages that nevertheless feel like lost homes.

I would apologize for these long digressions, for my reliance on reprises, for my failure—at times—to follow the thread, for my tendency to refract the lines of flight, for my insistence to evade recognition, even of myself.

The accompanying music video features scenes of Houston dancing in a setting of video screens and colored partitions.

Attracted to a mise en abyme *without* any hierarchically different levels: no subordination, only similarities—the text as a procession of resemblances.

On Etsy, you can buy a face mask with a customizable filter, personalized to match your own face. Other people want this. Over twenty people have this in their carts right now. On the street, the cheeks and lips contract to unnatural dimensions; tumescent, the chin swells, seems to swallow itself. One mask goes over the other, but in different proportions, as if I were a nesting doll, or the undivided set: a multitude.

I don't want to organize these thoughts. Is this an impulse to abandon narrative or to redeem it?

W says I am in love with being inside language, inside the act of writing. I think of these moments as a trans-action, where nothing gets restored and nothing gets exchanged, where things only multiply until they cut out, a simultaneity (excess?) that desires omission, that desires immersion. Notion of the *big glimpse*, not oxymoron but axiom.

> special skill: ability to feel out
> of place anywhere

I want to think about how my experience of time shifts, how time oxidizes and how this imperceptible reaction—a hyperawareness of passage, to slip into exactitude—occurs when and only when I am aroused.

This is the period of life in which such moments of which I have spoken are likely to come.

W describes it as *syntax-tumble* . . . my ability or inability to never stop on a point—to never land.

If asked about an ideal position, an ideal career, I would answer:

butthole surfer. Not, I think, a reference to the briefly popular nineties (actually formed in 1981) rock band Butthole Surfers. But a real, or at least hypostasized, butthole surfer. And I would picture the buttholes being surfed but especially the actual act of surfing, by which I'd glide, arms wavering at each side, each and every butthole that breaks against the shore. And then again, the *surf* of my intended profession could also suggest, not the act of lying on or over an ass so as to ride the cheeks—the groove between the buttocks, the visible and invisible borders between hip and thigh—but the mass or line of foam formed by such a recursive, rhythmic motion.

Notion of the "late bloomer." Or of being tardy, truant, wayward, and nevertheless, to germinate, in spite of this disobedience.

Instead of proposing an account of a specific future incident, the integration of logistics data into epidemiological models charts a series of futures. Virus, in other words, enacts an alternate temporal schema, a logic for reading a single moment through variable returns.

What's your mania? I imagine someone asking. What's your ideal setting for disintegration? Classrooms and hotel lobbies, art galleries, dinner parties . . . all occasions for opening, I'd say, multiple and repeating. I'd say, every space suffused with claims of ownership and purchase, a high degree of culture. The kinetic threat of a burglar approaching in plain sight.

(I am here the threat and also the one threatened by elegance and erudition, by a lifestyle and a language I can only ventriloquize in silence, stricken, wanting to become a single streak on the granite floor to which I will often direct my gaze for company in the event of absolute collapse.)

The idea of "finding one's self" (at any given moment) presupposes the loss of self as de facto metric.

Reading, too, is a kind of surfing, where I can glide across a current that would like to push me, dangerously, joyously, in various and conflicting directions.

In another book, I'd written: *I know that the hands can look, just as much as I know the pulse of every haptic glance I've given or received. Something stirs within me, just by looking. Just by being looked at. In ways that are closer to me than thought.*

In the margins of the paragraph, I write: *Every eyewitness necessarily implicates themselves. This text, too, wants to be put on trial.*

My inscription is too thick, launching violently into the center—I'm too excited, too excitable. The periphery penetrates the center; what's written penetrates what's printed; my copy becomes porous, almost illegible.

John Keats, speaking in the voice of someone else, wrote to Richard Woodhouse to tell him that poets are too busy filling other bodies to have an identity for themselves.

but to be gleefully stepped on
to be overtaken

& to be made aware
of this capitulation

not to all the others
with whom I am

near enough to touch but
self to self: to

know what I am
& to not have to

understand my desires for
continuous drilling / I liken

this cast of flesh to custom
& disguise / not so much

syndrome as unconditional
retreat toward the secrecy

of annotation
(so as to be here

twice) the point
of any interrogation

is to break, &
thus to be remade

reminds me of my recent
search history

where does the mouth end &
the lips begin

what is an ideal substitute for a face
& how should I listen

for history crossing
& uncrossing its legs

as when the inside & outside
switch places / as when

we fold the raw material
we wish to clasp together, to embrace

or make way for
the catastrophe

I was so excited to receive this, R writes, in their photo review of
the best-selling face mask with customizable filter. It is very beautiful and looks great on me! It helps to bring my face back to whole-
ness during this time of required face-covering. I'd love a smiling
one but will keep searching for that.

In solitude (Day 59), night is a substitute for day. I don't want to
prepare for my life, I feel like writing, I want to prepare for my death.

(He wanted a film that he could watch over and over and over again, so he began to play parts, to rehearse others for their own roles, to perform as a Director who was directing films. In this way, the films he directs will live in him. And the others, all the others . . .)

Equation of tree and speech as object. Equation of skinned knee and swing set as childhood memory. The smell of iodine, of charcoal pavement, of unmown grass, which I have had to forget.

(It's becoming nothing and everything.)

A former karate instructor named Peter Fitzek, who presides over a nine-hectare kingdom just south of Berlin, calls himself the King of Germany, of which there are many. Many Germanys and many kings.

At the roller rink in northern New Jersey where I had my first kiss, I stride below pulsing ribbons of neon, faceless necks and hands heaving tubes of dye and diphenyl oxalate at every entrance to the sleek oval track, which offers up the repetition of fantasy and the fantasy of repetition. I was four years old, maybe five. How many curving laps and how many glittering bodies have passed since then; how many first kisses begotten?

One thing I want to remind myself of is the usefulness of awe, wonder, and curiosity.

When someone can't remember another someone's name they say: *What's-their-face.*

In the movie I'd like to make, the scene would open on a wide two shot: passenger and driver in the front seats, the camera's eye facing the dashboard as the car moves, turns, stops (now and then, as when presented with a red light, or a roundabout). Each face would be partially obscured against a diaphanous frame replenished by the reflection of persons and objects the car passes. The couple would ride around in the middle of morning; we'd read the architecture of the city across each face. In this way, we see them, and also: we see what they see, as if the camera could teach us something about demolishing the boundary between skin and screen. In the movie I'd like to make, there'd be no difference between looking and being looked at, the gaze of the subject and the viewer, the narrative event and the event of narration.

I think that we should be more curious about our faces, about what our face gives and what our face hides, and what, in that surface obscurity, is given back or restored.

To measure the circulation within my brain, G places a transducer to my face, to the flesh above my ear. I like the part before—G's gloved hand applying a cool gel to my neck, my scalp, my eyelids—the best. Later, the instrument sends out a message to my brain, which my brain will or will not send back. When the energy reflects, the monitor to my left graphs the unit into colors, each hue (I guess) designating a different intensity. Sound turns into pictures, pictures turn into speed, when speed can be made material, returned as a body. Even if I couldn't look, as I'm looking now, I can hear it—the sound of waves breaking, or the beating of wings—collaborative incantation of the outside-inside, when the moment of coincidence turns into song. Waves on the shore, the flight of angels, or birds. Unless it's the swift ejection of a bomb, the long, slow descent. I want to keep it inside so I say nothing, except to ask about the name, to know the name of the instrument that makes art out of unseen breaths.

Notion of the momentary implosion, somewhere between image and after-image, whatever lingers and remains lodged in our pre-verbal consciousness to seep out moments or years later, a hovering that must necessarily remain virtual: neither *here* nor *there*.

Bad reading (reading for meaning, reading for completion) is like holding in a fart. But even worse, bad writing. On a whim, I ask a stranger on the street about holding things in, about the impulse or urge to hold in a fart. They say, because I'm so afraid of what might come out.

(As long as I don't *go anywhere* this text relinquishes all limitations.)

Rolling Stone described the song, which moves at a tempo of 120 beats per minute, as "perky synth-funk."

Fitzek's kingdom (Königreich), which is actually located in Wittenberg, has its own currency (Engelgeld, or *angel money*), its own healthcare and social security systems, and its own state-run bank, all of which is available for €390, or the current cost of citizenship.

Elsewhere, I had written that before the turn of the twentieth century, in the United States, there was no such thing as an undocumented immigrant. Or rather, every immigrant was undocumented. No legal documentation was required to move.

Let me clarify this further: the definition of who is here legally and who among us is deemed *illegal* changes as immigration laws change. To say you or your people came here—wherever here is—legally, that you migrated *the right way*, that you have nothing in common with those persons who came here without papers, is not just a matter of coincidence, or historical context, it's a lie. No one is illegal.

Today I would have asked my students to tell me about what stories haven't been written, about what was missing on their syllabi, about what was absent in their classrooms. I would have told them that neither my teachers nor the curriculums that they each abided by had ever accounted for the fact that by the end of the Renaissance, ambiguous bodies were translated as fixed and unchangeable; that medical practices involving the body were inextricable from the processes of colonial domination; that the pre-Columbian Americas, which had until then functioned as a space where undecided bodies and queer sexuality flourished, had to be converted to a European, cisgendered, heterosexual norm before they could be completely conquered. To talk about the colonial subject is thus to talk about the queer subject. And to talk about the queer subject is to talk about the subject who has been racialized, made mutable, fungible. We are talking, again, about the migrant, about migration.

And what happens, what is happening, when we shift the coordinates from which the locus of enunciation—the locus of knowledge production—occurs?

(In another book, called *A and B and Also Nothing*, I devoted a full page to a recipe for ropa vieja.)

Women are the carriers of culture, the ancestral past, which is so often measured by other means. I don't want to talk about a sense of familial and cultural unity through a colonizing language but through a culinary art . . . to return the past to the present, and to return a history of colonial trauma and acculturation to the body, to be ingested, savored; to transmute trauma as sustenance.

To write about what I long for can be a call to the past—what do I remember?—but also instructions for the future. What can I imagine?

There is a pleasure that is deeply sown in our bodies, from our bodies, and yet emanates as a collective force. To *desire* is to build but also to share. What gets exchanged is more than memory or imagination but the gratitude of community.

What is the difference between a desire and a need? Whether or not our ableist culture desires a dignity premised on care and compassion, our bodies have needs, and we should attend to our needs, and the needs of others, without compromise.

In school, in every creative writing class I took, my instructors would repeat something they themselves must have heard, must have been told, in turn: *write what you know*. But the knowing, the ontology of a Western positivism, isn't that the problem? When we write what we *already* know, we can only repeat ourselves, and everything, everything we've been raised to believe as historical, objective, rational fact.

W says I have a tendency to use semicolons and em dashes as commas or colons, to multiply a clause into vectors of constellation, to confuse subject and object, to muddle syntax, to mistreat (or overlook) punctuation, to dangle modifiers, to the extent that the reader may, more than once, lose their place.

(The body being looked at and the body looking. How we show ourselves to others and how we see ourselves in the act of showing and sharing: a heightened self-consciousness that moves us beyond reflection and toward reflexivity, beyond individual experience and toward group practice.)

Recognition and knowledge are two different things. I recognize myself in my work, the way I can recognize a stranger I've never seen before, a stranger I've never met. But I do not pretend to know what I've made, to be made aware, to be brought into that light that guides and that prevents us from seeing all the same or at the same time. Recognition is not knowledge. That's the first thing I want to remember to say.

The point of a sentence—isn't it?—is to get lost in it.

One of my earliest memories is of being tossed into the air, in Miami. Later, I'd swim underwater, darting between a set of outstretched legs, as if they were two ends of a tunnel. And it was nice, to not know whose bodies the legs belonged to, to be able to enjoy the body parts in their singular and mysterious beauty.

I like imagining Juliana in the mower's song. I like imagining what it is she exactly does to the speaker's thoughts, and how she does it, and when she does it, and how often. And what—I often probe— about the grass?

Every time I touch myself I am brought closer to a dividend I can never repay, which is a loss that is never or no longer *total*.

Just because we cannot get into the time(s) and space(s) that have been lived by another does not mean that we can escape them.

Was it Nietzsche who said that "I am all the names in history," or was it me?

[remember:] that a poetics of resistance can be a love poem; that pleasure and desire (the ability to imagine pleasure) is a resistance, and a resistance that is the celebration of life

[remember:] that after anger there will be, there is, compassion

(The body here is neither concealed nor enclosed; strictly speaking, it is neither hidden nor hiding.)

A related question: Can a text be both generous *and* resistant? Might this accommodation implore readers to attend to our own bodies, and our affective responses, as we pursue the text?

(The difference between *command* and *control* is a machine.)

I enjoy the moments when another's audio leaks out, to be shared publicly.

Notion of the accidental reveal, communal spillage, crowdsourced shame. Track the number of times a sequence repeats. Like water dripping. Or the zooming of cars, a fan, faces . . . to solicit your contribution.

Despite being unimpressed with the demo, Narada Michael Walden, who was then producing material for Aretha Franklin's album *Who's Zoomin' Who?*, came aboard, following some frantic urging by persons I will not here name. Walden's first maneuver was to request permission to change the song's lyrics and chord progression.

Even if we were in the same room, for example, the dimensions of the room would be different for each one of us.

It seems bizarre to zoom in on a face, rather than sitting around a table, M writes me, in an email. But teachers all over everywhere are doing just that, so it feels collective and not lonely.

Even before the requirements were put in place, I'd been wearing a mask. For weeks, months, years . . .

How often I've felt (without pausing long enough to register the feeling, to place it back—once cataloged—outside the body):

To be hailed differently in different spaces is a gift and a curse.

(Since the characters are shown facing in opposite directions, the viewer assumes that they are looking at each other.)

In mathematics, the *conditional probability* of an event B is the probability that the event will occur given the knowledge that an event A has already occurred.

The probability of A and B means that we want to know *the probability of two events happening at the same time.*

Yes is an acknowledgment or assurance, but also: an affirmation. We say yes to invite the actualized, the alternative, the imaginary into our lives.

To seek out an alternative to the vanguard party (to which I have declined all invitations), toward a rearguard, the arrière-garde (in an impossible language I still cannot pronounce), for the face that is hidden, but only because it chooses to hide. To take cover, then, which performs as both surface and substitute.

preliminary goal: to arrive at the table
leaking butt-play's cheery aftertaste

You discover things about yourself during routine moments shorn of their predictability. For instance, I had no idea what exactly my breath tasted like, at six in the morning, until I was forced to breath it back in, rhythmically, during my daily jogs.

If we admit what's right before our eyes—the fact of multiple presents, of a room that has been or is being presented in at least eleven other variations, eleven other arrangements—shouldn't we grant the past the same level of heterogeneity? If the present is a continuous interface, why not history?

I wrote jogs, not runs, because *daily runs* provides an impression of something I do not wish to pursue here. But what I do every morning, gliding across the grass on Ocean, can't exactly be called *jogging*.

And yet the complacency with which we move when we believe we are being directed by the hands of fate.

Fantasize, often, about getting hit by large vehicles, large bodies, elements too generous, too capacious to take or be taken by. Interest in collision as a textual behavior; picking up the pieces means piecing things together, to reconstruct what has happened, what hasn't happened. The shock of awareness brought by deviation and relief; recognition of turning the screw, of deranging or discomposing one's material. A deep deep sigh. And although I may be moving faster now, inventing accidents in order to discover something about an assumed origin, I still would like to set this text's time signature in the relatively slow rhythm of horseback, the short heavy motion of trotting, the monotony of tossing thoughts, of watching them revolve.

(I can leave in the middle of anything.)

M says translation is like learning how to swim. If you learn to swim then you swim with all your body, M says, and you want to swim a lot.

Members of the Reichsbürger movement (a subset of the population nearing nineteen thousand) believe that Germany (the federal republic) doesn't exist. Germany (the federal republic), they say, is a limited liability company controlled by the Allied victors of World War II.

If I don't look my age, is it me or the act of looking that is out of sync?

A jet just cruised over my head. I want to be the jet but also the head that sits, always under or below it; to cruise and be cruised, over or against something like the quarantined sky I have had to imagine.

Sometimes (although I don't know how often), the serialized repetition of pelvic thrusts, the joy of being overlapped and imbricated, pales in comparison to masturbation, which I liken here to the street insurgence of a childhood anecdote. To be rescued by the froth of what's unreturnable. Sometimes, rather than fuck L, I prefer to jerk off as L watches, in full view of my escape.

L faces me, as I pump my flesh sporadically, down and up, down and up, as if on a throne, or perhaps a reclinable beach chair, legs out and leaning, pausing briefly at the apex of the gesture, the cusp of my head—L faces me, but who do I face? It is the eye of the camera to which I seem to want always to direct my gaze, an audience that, by necessity, remains unseen. Not an audience, then, but the absence of one, which always implies their presence: plausibility as an engine of applause—etymologically, in parallel with an explosion—to drive off the stage by clapping. The same as when I write. Not the present—where I go when I want to get off—not even the future, but somewhere in between.

Don't mind if I cut out, J says. It's snowing here, J says, as if to remind us we're in different temperature zones.

If asked to remediate this alphabetical document, I'd picture it as a series of coordinates, or the waves and sounds that pass by each point at any given second. And is it or isn't it true that catching up with people who float in and out for hours depends on an attention to frequency?

For nine months and thirteen days, my Eustachian tube has experienced a dysfunction. I have a feeling, for nine months and thirteen days, of fullness, problems with balance. Sounds are muffled, like the chord is only halfway in the socket, like the image is not aligned with the audio track. Whenever I swallow, I hear a click running down my cheekbone, and I imagine being mechanically rewound, as if my lips were learning how to smile.

(A few years earlier, on a reality show, she'd demonstrated a favorite butt exercise, which consisted of writhing on the floor.)

No longer necessary to develop my photographs; it has become important only to keep taking them.

(Want to reach a point where *taking* supersedes or abandons all degree of ownership.)

In his attempt to find his namesake, he begins to impersonate him. And besides, he said, I was so keen to be in a film that I wished I had money to make a film so as not to disappoint you.

(Clicks, thumps, hiss, and hum were manually removed using Pro Tools HD. Crackle was attenuated using AudioCube's integrated audio workstation.)

What can be included among what was and continues to be lost, no longer available even after everything returns?

In another version of this class (to which we've each enrolled), I have written on the whiteboard:

MAKE A LIST OF SOUNDS THAT ARE NO LONGER WITH US

And scribbled in the margins:

IS IT POSSIBLE TO MISS A PLACE YOU'VE NEVER BEEN?

Knowing that to remember a place, one has to be reminded of the sounds that have been stored there.

I don't want to convince you of anything; I want to ask you questions while walking.

I heard to love cinema is to know what to do with the images that are really missing.

How can I bring myself to look at what I can't help seeing?

Cary Grant is talking to one of the anonymous factory workers; a tracking shot follows them along the assembly line. Behind them, piece by piece, as their conversation continues, a car is being crafted. "Isn't it wonderful!" This is what Cary Grant, or his character, the New York City ad executive Roger O. Thornhill, exclaims to the factory worker, or vice versa (the more I think about it, the more I forget who is talking to who, where the camera is stationed, and whether or not the factory worker is me). The two of us look at each other as we open the door to the newly minted car, or maybe right after we open the door, which is when (I'm certain of this) a corpse drops out. The characters walk off, into another scene, onto another set, never remarking on the question shared by every viewer subjected to such a horror: how a body can fall out of nowhere.

I know a work is done when I can't turn away, anymore, any longer.

But even more horrible: how a body can emerge out of absolutely nothing.

I've been working on a magic trick. It happens in the middle of morning the same as in the bowels of night. Each to each.

When the writing is good, we both disappear.

interlude /

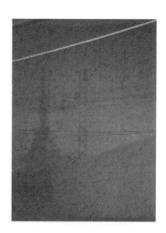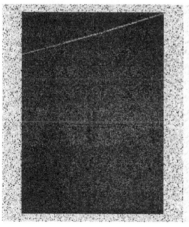

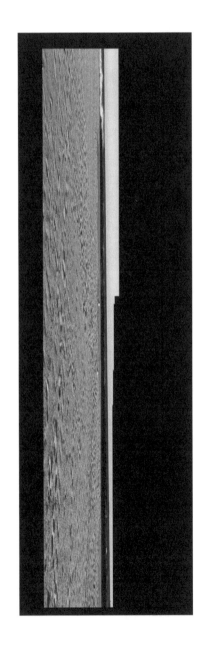

In the beginning was noise. And what was born was not a thing but its remembering: the memory of transmission. Your lips should be parted and slightly rounded. Remember to stick the tip of your tongue against the inside of your lower teeth. So this, I often watch myself say out loud, is how the face feels to speak French. In French, *parasite* may also refer to the static in a communication act, what we think of as interference, the often inaudible "noise" intrinsic to every transmission. A parasite, like the unintended interruption of information, forces a crisis, the etymological *turning point* that implies a change to the existing system or its pattern of relations. So a virus invades a body; so noise leaks out from the surface skin of a machine otherwise humming with the fiction of immediacy—in either case, what becomes exigent is adjustment, modulation, hospitality: the readjustment of our internal organisms as a means of survival, and a survival contingent upon copresence. In the company of virus, I am compelled to change, to surrender myself and my ideas about ownership and autonomy, to give up, and in giving up, to give myself, as nascent host, completely and unconsciously, over to my desiring guest. Neither subject nor object, *parasite* serves the artery of mediation, which provokes the passage of emergence: another I, whom I feel, in such moments, below my skin, as I learn about myself through the other.

The migrant, the human made illegal and alien, the asylum applicant existing between borders and nationalities, the undocumented body eliding the biometrics and data of surveillance and collection, the unreturnable exile, all of these persons appear to the state as

noise and parasites; all of these persons are articulated by the state
and its politicians in the language of plague and infection, as vector
of disease and contamination, as leech of social resources and
economic opportunities; all of these persons, neither subjects nor
citizens under the law, indistinct and unanticipated like the noise
embedded in every message, teach us about the limitations of the
state and the conditions in which it operates, the state of exception
that produces political legitimacy and legitimizes a politics of exclusion; the virus that is no longer a guest but a hostage: ransomed
and renounced, castigated and expelled.

What are the wider social and political consequences of the pre-
vailing logic—and desire—for immediacy? The aesthetic and political dimensions of omnipresent optimization, streamlining, and ra-
tionalization in our social and institutional spaces, our geographies
and ecologies, the precincts of law and governance, amidst the
time of pandemic and the amorphous spaces of the extraterritorial
camp? I am interested in the moment when noise infiltrates the
message and becomes a part of it. I am interested in the moment
two or more messages pass along the same channel. To be always
displacing the origin instead of restitching it. And still the endeavor
of tracing the fault lines, cracks along the edge of experience, vast
and vanishing. Varnished. This, too. The book as haptic ledger,
which accounts for the gradual impression of a body in space.
(Worthy of punishment; worthy of reward.) A hand reaching out
toward salt, toward sage and dust. A half-held torso tilting against
the breeze above a dune, in a photograph. In the past we'd say *a
picture book*. In the past we'd still use the present. I am right now
thinking about the etymology of the desert. Desert *as* etymology.
And so we track the variations. From barren, snow-clad mountains

to high-altitude asphalt. Pale gray eternity and neon-lit excess. We call it *the play of light*. Every generation has a tonal quality that'll be rendered in retroflexion. Color. Mood. Gesture of a hand: invitation to view this larger. The desert, which is always everywhere and nowhere, everything and nothing. And this because of the endless similarity of sand and sky, sky and sand; the repetition of a face, which is still loading.

a second (sequence) >

In the second part, there is a question:

which stories do I keep
in the words I collect?

At der Flughafen I waited for the S11 and watched the sun come up. A dark red almost purple sun breaking across the screen of my exterior. It was pleasure. Or at least that's how I responded moments earlier. That's how I answered when it was asked of me. My reason for being here. For being there. I said, pleasure.

For the last seven minutes I've watched another man circle the rim of his glass with a piece of citrus, squeeze the flesh, and tip it back. One, after the other.

Last night dreamt I met myself as a baby. Tears or the overwhelming feeling before tears as I looked at myself, sitting on the floor, incapable yet of walking. If I could speak, what would I have said to myself? And what would I say back?

While I take notes, I look at images. I can't tell—I don't know—if these images will survive the fraught process of publication, and so I would like to reproduce them here, to host their negative space as descriptions, like

silhouette of south Brooklyn at dawn, against an overpass,
moving across the BQE

The Sumerians understood that a dream should be recounted, recited as quickly as possible. The dream's magic power could alternatively be inscribed on a slab, the slab thrown in the river, to arrive elsewhere.

Always try to remember to look up, at 9:27 AM or a moment before, a moment after, to see the Gowanus Canal and a stretch of barren earth, mounds of dirt set against a site of pre-manufacture, pre-arrival, if I'm sitting in the corner seat and facing east. Something— but what?—long since gone, cannibalized to make a parking lot, or probably a pair of Targets. Role of the pedestrian remains to imagine everything we aren't already passing.

Would like to log the number of trains I just missed versus the number of trains that left just as I'd entered their sliding doors. Would like to map these findings, which are a form of loss, a mode of giving. In what subway stations am I least likely to miss my train? Which neighborhoods become waypoints for my perennial tardiness? And where—where am I going all this time?

ebb tide buffering at Brighton Beach (best viewed

At the airport, I am separated into a group of other people who are like and unlike me. Unlike because on the surface we have nothing in common, not even the same color eyes. Like because we are all wielders of the privilege that is citizenship in the United States. Elsewhere, the segregated lines that snake around the expansive room and spill out into a corridor, the stairwell from which it begins, mark nationality, but also something more, or something less, something citizenship forgets or elides: economic participation, social and gender and racial equality, the conditions of access and mobility. The lines don't exist to move bodies but to keep them in place.

by rotating the head

I am looking for a correspondence between events. Between then and now, there and here, imagination and memory, and the actuality of this transcription. In the gap between occurrence and its remembering there is a residue, not an excess but an absence, to the extent that it opens up or indexes something beyond us. Our role is to keep looking, at everything we can't see.

sideways)

(Half the image is streaked in the black sky of a machine's nervous energy.)

[remember:] error is utopic because it directs one to what is not; what could be; to accept something other than a limited and limiting truth

To the extent that words freeze in a text, it is only so that they might thaw and spurt by another's reading, whereby the combinations derived from particular times and spaces through which we enjoy each other necessarily exceed the page.

With unbroken waves of thoughtful detachment typically reserved for first dates, I watched the disembodied hands of women and men endlessly drawing and discarding the ivory tiles against the faint green felt surface in a game of televised mahjong. Thinking, as if a reflex, about the number of petals needed—their various mass, shape, hue; the density of air resistance—to smother so many unsuspecting dinner guests to death at a royal Roman feast.

I'm tired. Writing about a Kardashian interior already feels like writing about the void.

Is a book an object or an activity? I believe this reading requires a partner in order to take place.

(I realize I still have not said anything about the film from which this book's title comes. I haven't said anything, anything at all, except for the one scene that was never filmed. And perhaps we're still there. Perhaps that scene is now.)

In another photo, the artist has saturated a nonspecific building—all but a diagonal streak—in shadow. Vantage of a kitten looking up, from under the stairs, the way opacity actualizes release. Overexposed, as if color-corrected on film, there's a slab of windows, no curtains or blinds, a faint blur of cable-television chroma (among all the apartments) on the second floor, as if broadcast from another channel.

If asked to taste myself, as I oozed out of you, or just before, I would gladly tilt my head back, I would receive myself, which has been translated, in every sense, from your flesh. I would remark upon the discrepancies, the faint fulminations, the improbable particulars of what it was I was before you placed yourself, in your own way, inside of me, or the reverse. What I was before I passed through you. And after: to take the before (which has been altered, made plural) back in, gratefully.

+ the insistence not to have the last word (in any book bearing my name)

The books I like least are the ones that are too certain, too comfortable or clear about their own position and the conditions for the ideas they contain. The books I like least are rehearsing; the author rehearses the ideas they've already understood; the text tries to transmit a kind of understanding, which is knowledge, veiled in an argument. What I want is to try to work things out, and to be clear that I am (only ever) uncertain about the conditions for the work, which are always changing (just as I am), the thoughts and feelings I am only recognizing now (later) or that remain unrecognized by/unrecognizable to me. Can a mode of presentation that eschews argument and linearity for affinity and repetition return the *essay* to its etymological roots as an effort of movement? There is no commitment to completing a thought. I want only to keep having them.

(And we continue, indefinitely.)

A book lacks the gift of oral transmission, but this lack can be an invitation, for the reader to ventriloquize what is written, to put words in another's mouth.

(In the text we never forget that we aren't reading so much as being read to.)

My parents didn't go to school and so I think about them a lot as I navigate the institution and I feel like I am going to school for them but also that I am going to school *with* them, and so I feel like any time I write anything, that that experience, that story, is also theirs, that it belongs to all of us if it belongs to anyone. I often think about these things before I write and as I write and especially after whatever I'm writing is written.

Rather than a *non*fiction that is anti, absent, of little or no consequence, lacking the usual (especially positive) characteristics of the thing specified, or simply *other than* fiction, why not call this counterfiction? *Counter* as both complement and correspondence; and also: a level surface over which transactions are conducted, or nourishment is served, or on which goods are displayed or work is conducted.

I think of my genre as business/casual. I want to be serious. And I want to have fun doing it.

Possible synopsis: While collecting the scattered stories of his parents' entangled passages to the United States, the narrator begins to record the material onto videocassettes through a series of cutting and grafting, splicing footage of his present dislocation and overlaying on the audio track the polyphonic voices of his inherited exiles.

In a poll I conducted as I stepped out, for a walk, twenty-three people thought Cuba was in South America, seven people thought Cuba was in North America, thirteen people thought Cuba was in Central America. Three people couldn't tell me where Cuba was, or is, or where Cuba is going. One person, who doesn't need to be named here, didn't know where the Americas end, or begin, if all beginnings are subject to a plastic nativity.

(The geography of Latin American diaspora—the legacy of colonization and displacement and ultimately, dispersion—is irreducible to any discrete location.)

This tendency to leap into rumination's ether, break out into manifesto and then reconsider, retreat from thinking's calisthenics.

Our materials: the incidental, the quotidian, the earthy and everyday, the boredom—to carve space for the profound.

But duration or continuity, she said, can also be achieved by a very careful and dexterous manipulation of interruptions.

A text should be like a good seminar, where ideas are improvised and provisional, where learning happens through interruption and repetition, where similarities and resemblances are gleaned through shared geometry and second-hand retrieval. I leave class having learned that a lot of my own thoughts are not my own. I leave this text forgetting who it is who wrote it.

An incomplete list of things I aspire to be include a dental hygienist, a masseuse, a film projectionist, a soap maker, a sommelier, a body artist, a body double, a bar of soap, a Zumba choreographer, a follicle of hair, a great haircut from a new barber, a human resources associate, a clinical psychologist, a bellhop, an astronaut, a Chinese take-out sous chef, a receptionist, a teller, a babysitter, a

Gerber Baby, a sun god, a pseudonym, a grain of sand, a harvester of grains and barley (which is to say, a brewmaster), a Karate Kid, a drag racer, a cellist, a David Byrne impersonator, a hacker, a hologram.

How does the occurrence of event—its taking place: both the particulars of space and the unindexed potentialities of mobility—inform and shape the event itself?

I don't write books anymore, I write combinations.

If the function of the camera can be spoken of as the seeing, registering eye, then the function of cutting can be said to be that of the thinking, understanding mind.

I am curious about my own face; I take pleasure in that curiosity; I look at myself, my face, as if I were looking at the sidewalk, from the window, which I've just opened, to let the air in. And what happens on that porous surface can change at any moment.

(*Error* and *glitch* both originate in movement. To err is to wander; to glitch is to slip or skid off course.)

My job is only to produce coincidences.

What am I saying by saying that? I think I am saying that I'd like to think of this book as a compendium and the compendium as a combination, or a series of combinations. The one in front of me (in front of you) is only one combination, of which there are countless, countless . . . every time I read this out loud, the order changes. What I want is a book that doesn't end in publication, but begins here.

A combination can be an alliance of individuals united to achieve a social or political end. A combination is also an ordered sequence, such as a sequence of letters or numbers used to set a lock, or: to undo it. See also: the mechanism moved by the specific sequence.

How often I consider that eating is a matter of ethics as much as it is an act of eroticism—a body subtracted from the world, to be received by a(nother) body, and it all happens at the same time. I am drawn to concurrent experiences because they remind me I am not who I am, not all the time, or all the way. And what it means is only that I'm still moving. And that a look—every look—divides me into two, into multiples of two, into multitude.

To solarize a shot you reexpose it to light. Solarizing, then, is about exposing things twice. I maneuver my torso across the metal bars and lean in. On the rooftop, with a view of other buildings that rise higher, that resemble slate gray trees, I could be in any other city, it could be any other day. *August 21, 2017*

(I remember the date because I can look it up by looking up

When was the last total solar eclipse?)

Everyone in the city, at least everyone in the Lower East Side, where I walked from, and the East Village, which is where I am now, where I was when R was standing above me—providing instructions on how to carry myself, how to tense and where, and when, and how often, and close your eyes until I say so, until my words become quick bursts of concentrated light—was wearing thin cardboard glasses and turning their heads to the sky. It was as if, for one day, everything was inverted. People no longer looked down at the Cloud. We looked up, up, up, unafraid of losing our vision permanently, for the sake of something brief but absolute, something that will not be translated, something that we cannot render in a photograph, to place inside the 1:1 aspect ratio, to be deposited into the landfill of moving images.

If this is a reprise it is arranged as a perpetual canon (canon perpetuus). And what turns up here, what becomes apparent, even briefly, what I wish to hold (and so I pause this combination), what I am trying to attune my senses to, what I want to be attentive to, what I am striving to make out, what splits from all these differences is what musicologists call *the catch*.

Establishing a chain of equivalence in the text means also turning particular subjects into (an) empty signifier/s.

Just as the naturalization process has been shown to produce a discourse of otherness at the same moment that it grants the right to belong, the asylum system has been understood as a generator of new-old essentializing constructions of sexuality that function within nationalist logics. By *new-old* I mean the antiquated aspect of "immutable" sexuality that persons must revive and, later, reaffirm, to gain asylum based on being persecuted for their sexual orientation.

(Remember to look at the ways in which asylum testimony risks re-inscribing the same structures of inequality from which applicants seek refuge.)

The double-bind offered by asylum is to produce a testimony that will grant you legal residence while also fueling racist, homopho-bic, and colonialist relations that will be detrimental to your newly "protected" life.

What is the difference between a border and property, property and a prison?

(Space enters history through the prevention of motion.)

And is it or isn't it true that police officers, in tandem with predic-tive policing, are not so much serving the prevention of crime as the production of threat? And is it or isn't it true that law enforce-ment and the academy and the municipality work hand in hand?

I don't want to command, I don't want to prescribe, I don't want to convince you of anything; I want to ask questions. And listen for the mark that curves like an earlobe or a flash of lightning, like one letter swaddled over another.

slip & slide (as title & method?)

When watching an eclipse, you must wear eclipse glasses at all times if you want to face the sun, a woman's voice announced, hours earlier, when I was still in a bedroom, lying on a bed that wasn't mine. Or, she droned, as static cut through the frequency, as I pulled my legs up to my chest and wet my lips, use an *alternate indirect method.*

(The short time when the moon completely obscures the sun is known as the *period of totality.*)

And if this is done by the same person who is shooting, there will be a minimum of footage which ends up, or should end up, Maya Deren adds, parenthetically, in the trash basket.

What if the point is not to minimize the trash but to collect it?

And as I walk (while listening) I will often look back.

In the spring of 2017, I wrote a book by sampling Gertrude Stein and Henry James. I laid my voice on top of theirs to say something about what it means to be [an] "American." Or what it means to be outside the system of legibility.

(Dissimulation as *hiding with words*)

alternate indirect method as (alternate) title & method?

The book begins the moment I walk in from the narrow hallway; the moment I sit down, surrounded by other students; the moment you introduce yourself; the moment you ask us to introduce ourselves to one another; the moment you give us your only set of instructions. And the rest is a meandering, toward no obvious or intended destination. The book becomes a passage into an experience along the phenomenological divisions between fact and fiction, distraction and concentration; the book wants to wander into chance encounters but also toward the interventions that it self-consciously tries to stage. It is a story about coincidences but also permissions and occasions: about what is invited and what isn't and why that is and what can be done what can be done for those of us without an invitation. If there is such a thing as "plot," I want it to be dictated by association.

To be in that classroom—to be the first in my family to be there—it was an experience of honor and an honor that was a betrayal. That recognition and shame could be linked, that recognition and shame were not opposites but interdependent—a realization which, like all things, I am still undergoing.

I alight upon a line I remember writing, which is to say a line I remember reading: *Elsewhere, I found success* because *of semblance; just enough of nothing to be any body.*

And in the margins, I've written: *just enough of everything to be nobody.*

In an earlier version of that earlier book, there was a playbill. It looked, unless I'm remembering this wrong, like this:

Henry James	*writer*
Gertrude Stein	*writer*
Henry James	*character*
J (multiple)	*characters*
S/Z	*character*
Christopher Newman	*character*
CC	*character?*
L	*character*
K	*character*
C	*character*
G	*character*
M	*character*
H	*character*
W	*character*
E	*character*
Americans	*ensemble cast*

(This book has become an annotation of another book.)

When I first recited this book, before it was a book, when it was (only?) a presentation on last week's reading material, another student told me there was a name for what I was doing. They called it *middle-distant reading*.

I must have misheard them, or written it down wrong, or my classmate invented what it was I was doing because *middle-distant reading* became *middle-distance reading* when, on the F ride home, I searched the term and found 5 Different Types of Reading Glasses for Different Tasks, and several other similar articles, or advertisements.

And totality, I had heard, I recalled, was the only safe period of viewing, of taking in. Safe safe safe, and boring, and a lie.

(I never get high except for that photo.)

Isn't all writing excess? Doesn't all writing arrive only as supplement, but also difference: the result of withdrawing, recalling, deduction?

Despite or maybe because of the playbill, other characters began to emerge.

> writing always comes after
> & at the same time
> writing never catches up

Laying my body against the cold cushion of the medical table, a magnetic field temporarily realigning my water molecules, I felt the waves pulse until I had become a part of the pulsing, until flesh was indistinguishable from the sonic objects drumming against flesh.

Writing a book is nothing if not an experience of waiting. You wait for the text to take over, to be returned, to teach you something.

(Toward an avant-garde that prefers to come from behind.)

While the head of MI6 (the UK's Secret Intelligence Service) is still referred to as "C" today, the Director General of MI5 has not been known as "K" since the 1940s.

Consider how this version of the avant-garde—double-facing; drawing from the front, approaching from behind—could *only* be produced in movement, the traversal between geographies and generational epochs, where "border-crossing" serves as more than metaphor but as methodology and autobiography.

People also ask: Can MI6 agents tell their family?

If common conceptions of diaspora privilege an origin—as well as an undetermined degree of distance—then what is enacted by this mode of creative expression is not the search for source or singularity but a commitment to waystations and shared differences. What happens when we recalibrate the terms of visibility and the logic of Western universalism?—not to make everything available (that is to say: visible, sortable, graspable, consumable) but to convert the well-rehearsed historical past into the realm of the unspeakable; to silence the dominant and dominating narrative of history, as well as modernism's reification of cultural difference through primitivism, such that affective experience serves quiet contemplation in place of visual (de)termination and binary thinking. What other histories emerge? What futures?

Common greeting, as we enter or appear, as we alight upon one another, even in passing: *I'll be with you in a moment.*

These are only some moments in which consciousness seized me.

Or that I was seized by distraction and anticipation, the urge to be doing—to be thinking—something else.

C says I say words like it's my first time saying them. You are sounding out the word, C says, at the same time that you are speaking it.

My advanced reading copy of *Creative Gatherings* includes a four-page correction sheet with the typewritten instructions: *When you receive this book, please make these changes.*

Because there is history, there is absence. Another way of saying this is: There is history *because* there is absence.

I was asked to write a short composition about what happened to me and about my first impressions of the United States. It is very difficult to really answer such a question because my experiences and feelings are so many and widespread that I could not describe them within the frames of a short story.

If asked to explain the *Also* of the title *A and B and Also Nothing*, I would mention that the book is also an attempt to theorize a hybrid poetics that doesn't depend on the academy for its own mythology. That I was striving to connect the multiple and heterogeneous experiences of "hybridity" and to think about how the best indicator of its social and political value was not, as composition and rhetoric theorist Patricia Bizzell has written, its employment by "powerful white male scholars" in academia, but through its everyday mobilization by people of color, by people of mixed races and ethnicities, by people who do not conform to gender norms and body norms, by people who have experienced disability throughout their lives, by people who are in this place without being of this place. How the legacies of migration, exile, and displacement could be a dedication.

Majoritarian culture's desire to pinpoint the locus of hybridity, and in failing, to desire to negate it, is exactly the point. What we want (desire as our resistance) is to implore a system of value, a method of knowledge production, that resists accumulation and ownership. Rather than emphasize the hierarchical parent-offspring structure of Bizzell's genetic interpretation, I would like to redirect the effects of hybridity toward a framework in which previously disparate moments, languages, people, and places are observed through another lens of connectivity, with intricate, often haphazard exchanges, where what is produced is not a chronology but an interval.

In the white, white West-world in which I live, I wield such a privilege to pass, to move, to negotiate different boundaries, the way J was able to do, upon arriving in New York City and eventually moving up the ranks from the mailroom to the line, as a lending officer. He was lending out his experience with credit without giving up anything of himself, not all the way or not at all, passing himself off to clients and strangers—even his girlfriend's mother, my would-be babcia—as Italian, in the wake of anti-Cuban rhetoric and the Bay of Pigs invasion. What is credit but something derived from enjoying the confidence of another? And the provision—isn't it?—is always with a view to the future. I didn't pass myself off, J corrects me today, when I read him what I've written. I just didn't correct anyone, their assumptions. Dissimulating? I ask. Dissimulating? he echoes. Pretending to not have, I return, to not be, what you are.

And it's important for me that the reader looks—it's the looking that matters.

> apparently you can
> fix any cheek
> sucked-in selfie
> by inserting a
> plate of pasta
> under the lack
> of opening
> of the lips
> spaghetti seems
> to work best
> for turning pouts
> into gestures of joy
> & anticipation

(In an animal communication study of capuchin monkeys, the *duck face* term has been used synonymously with *protruded lip face*, which females exhibit in the proceptive phase before mating.)

> the erotic horror of looking
> at a stranger's spam folder
> is it or isn't it

true / urge
only alights
as a thing known

when it goes
unsatisfied? I
mean to be made or make

pleasure into artificial
necessity
thus an urge

speaks only of
its own absence
its own presence

to be the urge then
not the one feeling
or being felt nor

the body eaten
nor the act itself
neither object nor

its adoration

"I ask of writing what I ask of desire," Hélène Cixous writes, "that
it has no relation to the logic which puts desire on the side of possession, of acquisition, or even of that consumption-consummation

which, when pushed to its limits with such exultation, links (false) consciousness with death."

Recurring dream in which I'm trying, desperately, to jerk off in public. This dream converges with the "I'm naked in public" dream (so common, so boring) so that I don't know what comes first: the fact of my nudity on full display or that I wanted to masturbate, so I took off all of my clothes.

When I am dying, will I be *beyond things*? Pain, pleasure, heartache, disappointment, lust, envy, a certain kind of hunger? A certain kind of regret? The emblem and the art of it? The strength or lack of it, the cruel ambition? The fear and the freedom of a deep intimacy, a deep deep vulnerability—the setting for me to be, and for me to be finally *myself*.

I fantasize about a correction sheet inserted, too, in this book, which, like all books, should necessarily remain uncorrected.

To change the shape of a face requires cutting into the jawbone and I couldn't decide whether resting my left arm or my right on the table better conveyed "maximum desperation."

If I didn't have to go on living, he said, and were courageous enough, I'd have liked to be hanged from the beams of cinema.

(Artificial aura of a swimming pool pulsating against the dark. The lone light laminating the cool blue chlorine dream of evening. A single woman. A single moon scotch-taped to a muted wall.)

"But they become more and more difficult to organize," Cixous says of her daily profusion of notes, "where are they going to find their adequate place inside the text? So I use an enormous amount of small signs, stickers, etc., in order to try here or try there, just to see whether they adjust or not."

Texts, too, adapt to their users' language and experiences. Think of Google Maps, which requires and relies upon a similar bespoke cartography, fundamentally altering our reality by trading in public space for a global vision of the world that is different for each user.

(Only when you enjoy taking selfies will you have the confidence to take more, she explained.

And only when you look pretty will you enjoy taking selfies.)

The Japanese, I later learned, call it *kodoku*; the lonely gap in between the real me and the masked me.

People began to adore their image, not for what it was but for what it wasn't, which was them, unadorned and unadulterated. So entranced by the face that had been given back to themselves, they wanted to let the digital dream leak out into the everyday life of birds and trees; they'd show surgeons their doctored digital selfies, printed out in low-grade ink. Turn me back into myself.

Or maybe: Make me become what it is I resemble and what I can never be, beyond the provisional web of re-presentation. Not a question but a command. Was it Wittgenstein who said the limits of my language mean the limits of my world?

(CC isn't me but it is also everything I have become.)

The perfect search engine would be like the mind of God, said Google cofounder Sergey Brin, shortly after the company's initial IPO, in 2005.

In soap operas, whenever the script called for drama, they'd frame my face in an awkwardly accelerating close-up, a precursor to Instagram's superzoom feature, whose popularity, I think, is tethered to our appetite for unnatural immediacy. Eater of all imagination, each lens at any given time plunges. Erratic, but for the preordained arrival against my unblinking eyes, the mouth slightly ajar, my white teeth, for which I paid extra. Incapable of understanding the depths of other people's desires, the craving to live inside or die into the fleshy expression of disorientation or dread to which others could merge their low-level weekday afternoon trauma, I never knew how long to hold my practiced gaze; how long until the scene, mercifully, would dissolve. Because none of these programs used a studio audience, I was permitted, as I looked into the eye of the camera, to imagine my own face looking back, a doubling only made possible through omission. On the internet, you can see a montage of my deadened complexion in rotating scenarios, just by typing my name in YouTube's search bar, giving *perplexity* or *sangfroid* or maybe only fear.

Moving through days with the knowledge that faces that do not conform to the schema fashioned by environment and experience and the morphologies of racialization can only be perceived in pieces.

Remember how images of humankind (both man-made and machine) make and unmake us into simultaneous creator and created, embodied and interpreted, authors and inscribed, and the insecurity the regime of surveillance determines and is determined by.

What does it mean to be "camera-ready" in a world where cameras, too, have been integrated with our bodies?

I made an inner "click" and recorded the scene, although I don't know why.

Remember the link between the normalization of videoconferencing and FaceTime and the rise of jawline reconstruction in the United States.

When I got my new face, I said, they never told me I'd inherit the memories that passed before it.

The following is a partial list of unproduced Alfred Hitchcock projects, in roughly chronology order:

> *Number 13* (1922)
> *Forbidden Territory* (1933–1934)
> *Greenmantle* (1939–1942)
> Unnamed Titanic project (1939)
> *Escape* (1940)
> Unnamed Nazi documentary (1945)
> *Hamlet* (late 1940s)
> [the list continues for several more pages]

What else is brought or arrives by the refusal to make distinctions between fiction and history, between sound and image, between subject and object, between viewer and viewed, between body and screen?

If I showed you a page from my notebook you'd say: *Sometimes you'd think he'd never used a camera before.*

> one patient describes destroying
> every image she has found
> of herself before her
> surgeries began / the beauty
> of pictures taken before
> the digital age: each massacre
> of the past is final & thus gone
> for good

(If the desert is a magnet, it is also a vacuum, and the best art is the kind in which the material abandons its canvas.)

In metaphysics, A series and B series are two different descriptions of the temporal ordering relation among events. In the A series, events are ordered as future, present, and past. The essential characteristic of this series of temporal positions is *continual transformation*, in the sense that an event here is thought to be first part of the future, then part of the present, then part of the past.

The assertions made according to this modality correspond to the temporal perspective of the person who utters them.

Remember President Harry S. Truman, who, after committing troops to Korea under United Nations command, told a reporter who'd asked for further clarification: US presence will amount to no more than a "police action."

On the fourth day of the war, bombing attacks are for the first time approved by an aggressive party glossed in the costume of humanitarian servant, in the war that is not a war in a country that is no longer recognized as such. Every week for six weeks, the police action aspiring to provide "relief [to] the Korean Republic to suppress a bandit raid" increases its intensity; on August 26, the US Air Force drops eight hundred tons of bombs on North Korean cities, an operation that repeats every day, without cessation, until November 3, when the daily bombing quota of eight hundred tons increases.

At the neurologist, weeks after a second scan of my brain, when the doctor looked up from her papers as if reading from a script to tell me that it was highly likely, given everything we know, that I was not dying. I cry. On a compact disc, each cross-section of my brain like slices in a loaf of bread. My mother's hand holds me. Not my hand but my whole being. How small I had become. So I shook in that stiff chair with my head bent, sobbing into my free hand and secreting mucus freely onto the sweater I had worn for the occasion. Out poured more tears than I had allowed myself to shed since my symptoms began, another lifetime or another life. Not because I was dying but because I was not dying. Because I wanted for once and all at once to make it stop. For the dread to leave me, even if it came at the expense of the body that had been wrecked by it.

Why do I confess (to you)? When already you know (everything)?

"Burn it if you so desire. Not only that, Strat," the letter reads, "but burn and destroy as a lesson to any other of those towns that you consider of military value to the enemy."

(On behalf of the war that is not a war; the war that never formally ended; the forever war.)

In the B series, events are ordered according to a different mode of temporal positions by way of two-term relations that are asymmetric, irreflexive, and transitive: earlier than (or *precedes*) and later than (or *follows*). In other words, if an event ever is earlier than some events and later than the rest, it is always earlier than and later than those very events. Events here are no longer continuous but static.

Attracted to the work that begins to organize itself (independent of authorial control or generic construction). The aim of what we call "art" seems so often to be this retrieval or retribution of cultural memory, cultural unconsciousness: the micro-story, the marginalia, the errata, the anecdote. Things change when they land in a book.

I stop ~~reading~~ writing so I can look at photographs of myself. I stop writing to look at these photographs and as I look, as I keep looking, I consider how writing is an attempt to give voice to the images, to make an audible image. What else is the "I" on the page but another apparition, a replica that speaks?

When I was twenty-three or twenty-four, R told me to make sure I tell others (all the others) that I hadn't done anything before I did Levi's. R said: Make sure you tell them I discovered you. R's point, I think, was that everybody is entranced by the origin story, but even more, by the origin story that has no origin. Put another way: we like (am I including myself here?) the miraculous feat of immaculate conception: to come from nothing. Tell them, R said, you haven't done anything. I hadn't done anything, I thought then, like I'm thinking now. But I never do nothing.

My favorite part of any conversation, when I'm talking to a robot, is something else. Something else, I'll say, when asked what I'd like to accomplish, where I'd like to go.

Today a student dreamt of a drone that would follow them, broadcasting back their body and face in real time. So they could see what it was they looked like to others. So they could see what the others saw or see, which is another way of saying: so they could see themselves as if they were anyone else.

"Hold still," Cixous laments, "we're going to do your portrait, so that you can begin looking like it right away."

The expression "to save one's face" comes from the Chinese phrase *tiu lien*—to suffer such a public disgrace so as to be unable to show one's face in public; to lose one's face. Saving face means preserving dignity. Dignity means maintenance, a balancing between a person and a model, life and the norm—conformity, the appearance of *always being in one's place*.

The only tragedy available to me was in my spam folder. Here, she said, leg bent, leaning against the masking flat, is where I could live out love, lust, heartache, bankruptcy, passport snafus, and the devastation of a message from the mailer daemon.

(Spam's origins in displacement are not coincidental.)

> I ask you to eat me
> while I'm still breathing
>
> in this way I know I've been
> wanted

Isn't it possible that we would like to be both visible and hidden? Private and public? Vulnerable and guarded? Above all to be seen without being known or known without being seen or each of them simultaneously, despite or maybe exactly because one so often obviates the other. To see redirects a radical intuition. To know means to close one's eyes to finally apprehend what's behind the image. What's underneath it. What's inside or at the very bottom.

(We came forward, softly.)

The artist as patient (able or willing to bear) & patient (one that is acted upon), who catches bacteria & waits for it to take shape—a new form for the body, a modification, a shift in organism or its organization—to promote risk. To run toward imperfection & error the way I run toward my own sickness—to become sick with my own body—this is to be sick with my own existing form & to want to develop it, to heighten or degrade it, to cross-section it & see what leaks out of each measureless incision: the world. What do I want but to infect & become infected by you. & you. & you. & you. & you. & you. & you. & you. & you. & you. & you. & you. & you. & you. & you. & you. & you. & you. & you

(When resuscitated during pandemic, this note admitted an altered glaze.)

Memes, deepfakes, sex bots, and direct messages-as-intimate-encounters are not merely cultural narratives, but virtual constructions designed to concretize in unintended ways. Post internet axiom: it is not reality that creates the internet but the internet that creates reality. In this Möbius strip what unfolds is not the reverse of reality but its continuous permutation. I used to think of such moments as *generative fictions*. But aren't all fictions generated and generative? To the extent that they bring us closer to the truth, even if what's true is the presence of surface, when surfaces no longer conceal but permit. The "real" is always lost in any representation; in fact, to begin with, it was never here.

The screen splits down the middle, so you can see both of us and the ways we converge or won't we.

(I stopped writing because [I realized] my eyes were closed.) I want to tell you how hard it is to keep my tenses consistent. I want to tell you how hard it is to know if this is still happening, and if it is, [when] will it stop?

Last night I had the strangest dream. I sailed away to China in a little rowboat to find you.

And you said you had to get your laundry cleaned. Didn't want no one to hold you. What does that mean?

(In the novel, everyone talks only in song lyrics.)

And if the modulations of wind and rain played on in this memory of our encounter to which I can and cannot begin. And if you knelt beside me. If you held me until I burst with fragrance and fruit I cannot name. If you reached your hand below my chin and if I pushed my head down, if I placed your hand here. (For me to lick.)

The song then explodes into its beginning, with myriad locations and various outfits by Houston, while dancers try to impress her as she treads air. Toward the finale, she manhandles a guy, who dons a look of shock and surprise, asking him, "Don't you wanna dance, say you wanna dance?"

Readers—I'm not sure how many—thought it strange that a writer would ever work as a model, but aren't all writers models? In the sense of our attendance to the movements demanded by a pose—to present, to affect, and even to oppose, through careful reproduction. What is writing except the means of display, and also: a system for displacement?

A surface can be a space for massaging; to massage others onto a surface (of one's own body) is to lubricate, while retaining a necessary friction.

In his review of *Whitney*, Jon Pareles of *The New York Times* offered a mainly negative appraisal, writing that listening to "I Wanna Dance with Somebody" was like "watching television while someone fiddles with color controls."

Do you remember the lighthouse in Otranto? We'd cast our gaze over the water, pretend we knew which way was east.

It had been a strange month. The temperature had risen and then dramatically dropped; south Brooklyn was draped in a haze that lasted most of the week. The humidity increased. And at night, when I'd walk under so many streetlights, the air had that rare quality of resembling a movie set. I'd stroll, or glide, as if under a strobe, my vision caught between a jarring brightness and the opacity of the sky; footage of the eighties movie I was watching, or in which I was one of its numberless characters.

Because I want to escape into my counterpart, I keep reading. And I read everything: storefronts, billboards, signals from passersby I've never seen before.

Is the word I'm looking for *quiver* or *swell*?

I write down the lines of the entire film, M explains. What each character says. We always say lines from some of our favorite films, and we kinda thought, why don't we do those films, why don't we be those characters?

I want to say something else about the reprise, which is also like wanting to say something about the interval (between what is happening now and what might be).

material (of the past) vs./& its manipulation (at present)

I am curious about the particular charge brought by the anonymity of the material and the partial erasure of its original context.

While working on an interpretive dance number about the unproduced films of Alfred Hitchcock, the narrator spots his double on the street. He [predictably] becomes obsessed with this double and has several more run-ins with him until they

The detail as both omission and obsession. (It is a question of scale.)

Instructions or memoranda: Pick at least two texts. And then film your experience of reading these texts, while the reader watches.

There's a moment in the book, the book that was not so much a translation as it was a story about translating, a moment in which I list James, Stein, Sontag, de Certeau, Duchamp, Deleuze, Derrida, Lacan, Nelson, Pasternak, Kraus, Klee, Barthes, Berger, Burroughs, Benjamin . . . all in a single sentence, one after the other, like a police lineup, except I was not incriminating them; by placing them together in my work, by reciting them as my sources, the people I had been taught and the people I've learned from, I was incriminating myself.

(I saw these strangers as friends and these friends as accomplices.)

In every book, I like to add a section at the very end devoted to citation, devoted to the lineage of the text. Another way of saying this is: I am giving you a kind of source code, and I'd like you to do more than retrieve the data, but re-write the program.

A game I like to play—don't you wanna?—is to name one Black or brown or Indigenous avant-garde theorist. More points* if you can name a Black or brown or Indigenous avant-garde theorist who appeared on any number of the syllabi you received while in school. More points if you can name a Black or brown or Indigenous artist taught in any class on the avant-garde. More points if you can name a class—any class—devoted to the Black and brown and Indigenous avant-garde.

Remember Aubrey Williams, the Guyanese artist who converged postwar European abstraction with ancestralism, contemporary science with pre-Columbian symbols and imagery. Williams—who led the early Caribbean Artists Movement in London—not only countered the either/or of the abstract and figurative but also confronted national and nativist leanings, resisting the romanticization and exaltation of Indigenous culture within the landscape of the West Indies, while desiring to locate his own body of "the unrecoverable" through a current of Latin American art that connected

---

* But who's counting? And what is a "high score"? Or rather: what, here, would constitute a "win"?

North America with South America and the Caribbean. Remember Roberto Matta, from Chile; Rufino Tamayo, from Mexico; Wifredo Lam, from Cuba. Remember that any question of representation is a question of ecological belonging and hauntological trace; a question of rupture that is not final but formative, when "aftermath" is not finite but reoccurring.

In Spanish, *citar* can refer to an appointment or arrangement; to be anointed or assigned to, to plan for an eventual encounter.

(Not what I expected. A little taller. A little more polished than the others.)

With such expert playacting, P says, sitting down on a couch, crossing his legs, two fingers on his temple, you make this very room a theater.

I take a break and return. I imagine that while I am away, I am actually with you. And when I return (and because I return), I repeat myself.

I am working through a question of location settings: the places and conditions in which one's body becomes an object of the state apparatus, the technology and teleology that facilitates this rendition—which is always an act of translation, surrender, and extraction, without the requirement of return. I have been working through it my whole life, the way I've inherited, more than anything else, I think, the effects of each of my parent's exile.

Traces sometimes don't bear a source, but only more traces.

And every repetition is like an assertion but also a hesitation . . .
I am repeating a thought, not because I am certain of the idea
coalescing within it, but because I am completely uncertain. I am
uncertain of myself.

(I bring this up to clarify my uncertainty.)

How it could be an honor and also a betrayal, and how both of
these things mattered dearly to me; both of these things weighed
heavily upon me—I felt both of these things pressing in on me, and
that the pressure of deformation was turning me into something I
did not yet know and still don't know fully. That of the honor of
being a first-generation citizen; that of the betrayal of leaving the
naturalized family, of escaping for the infinite (which is knowledge,
or the illusion of knowledge in the institution, a gated community
that was closed off to all, to all in my family but me).

Remember: the body expands—it always blows up a little—right
before it decomposes.

(Certain pleasures emerge from duration and accretion.)

The fantasy of every writer: to switch places with their reader.

(The old familiar anxiety of abstraction, which asks me whether
I am looking at the page the right way up. Whether I shouldn't
rotate the book, re-read re-write what it is I've written read.)

I think of each paragraph as a moment of consciousness briefly tethered to language / there is no distinction between more fully formed "thoughts" and the gleaming of their articulation.

At some point I came to understand something about myself, or at least my work. I didn't want to tell stories. I wanted to describe the experience of stories entering the body. I wanted to tell you what it was like to be me. In the hopes that you would also feel what it is like to be you.

If I were to write a sequel, or spin-off, or companion to the book on American identity, which was as much or much more a book about migrant identity, I'd want to return to the subject of aesthetics, to a textual structure that configures the political through its formal properties. And I would want to consider how a hybrid poetics is not so much a choice as it is a response, and the response a remainder: not just an expression of the isolation and alienation of a body that does not comply to various norms but also an expression of joy, and a joy that is a celebration, and I'd want to clarify that this celebration runs deeper, deeper, deeper.

Nothing comes from nothing but to understand that we would need to take seriously the unintended proposition of Edward Said, or to read, rather, his statement in "Reflections on Exile" at face value: "because *nothing* is secure." We would need to take him at his word, whether or not he meant that security might be found in the insecurity of negation, disavowal, effacement, the incompletion of transition, of incohesive transit.

(My non-arrival of diaspora, the indelible mark of *cubanía*, to be recognized and to recognize what it is to be now here and not from here and also to be never here, an entanglement that ruptures the logic of individuation.)

[remember:] what is unrepresentable is not the same as what is an alternative to representation

Reversible model (under capitalism): multiculturalism as narrative trope of the state, not its people; the espousal of celebrated diversity systematized under one flag.

Globalization as obliteration, not expansion. Instead of multiple, heterogeneous temporalities, we have instantaneity. Instead of a rich diversity of ethnicities and cultures, we have multiculturalism.

How can I explain this or can I explain this (even to myself). To be mixed is to feel as though you look like no one but yourself, and at the same time, to recognize so many others, so many strangers, that could be just like you. Thank goodness for people, for all the people I will never know, to remind me who I am and what I came from.

In the book that came before this one, I'd written: The pursuit of form is really the pursuit of time, because it is always the form of a work that informs its duration in your mind's eye—the time you require to spend together in undissolvable hospitality.

And what I meant, or what I mean now, is that it is because writing, like reading, is an experience of duration that the text, like its author, has undergone so many changes between when I started and whenever, whenever I'll decide to turn my head, to look up, to look away.

(Like any good film, we never forget we are reading when we are reading this back.)

I was raised by two communist wolves, the last cub to enter the pack. We shared everything we owned and wore. This is why I never found things and clothes useful. This is why I'm so used to being naked.

A book that sheds value like information post-publication: textual entropy.

I feel exactly this, I think, in publication, or just after: the sense of being outmoded immediately upon arriving. Perennial belatedness as a cultural condition (a temporal caesura) no matter what it is one is producing or how.

(I was asked to write a screenplay around "an original idea" Hitchcock had "carried in his head" since the late 1930s.)

If asked about my other aspirations, I would include the wish that my jeans remain unzipped; I would observe that this text wants only to continue to remark upon other texts (that are similarly in progress . . .): something always to look forward to, and for the text to cultivate that imaginative landscape. What other goals should a book have but that? I often think.

+ lavishing oneself with the limitations of translating English to English, and the arrogance or ignorance of writing about Henry James and Gertrude Stein after a week's worth of reading their work. The arrogance and ignorance of remaking this film that remains paused at the three-and-half-minute mark.

I write for all my dead friends and mentors. And especially for the ones who are still alive. Who are still here, who are present in this text, who present themselves to us again and again . . .

> I heard trace
> is the insertion
>
> of words
> in time

(Two angels hear/see/watch over everything. But not all thoughts

have wings. And so they can't get inside the people they preside over. They can only learn by looking.)

Clint Eastwood and Sean Connery were possible male leads. Liv Ullmann was asked to play the double agent's wife. Catherine Deneuve was also asked to star. Walter Matthau was considered for the villain role. Ed Lauter was also discussed for a role as one of Matthau's cellmates.

It is worth reminding myself: borders are parameters that can be negotiated.

(The difference between *ice cream* and *ass cream* is only a slip of the tongue.)

And in re-writing the American I intentionally or unintentionally re-write the nation to which we pledge allegiance, or rather the fact of our pledging. What I want, I'm thinking now, like I thought then, is to absolve ourselves of our fidelity to emperors and adventurers, all sovereigns, kings, and leaders, so we can become whatever it is we were born to be.

What is an engraving but an indistinct notion or remembrance,[†] or an act of communicating through another source? And when we *scratch things out*, we produce a text through just this series of alterations, the pressure of stamping and pressing, the meeting of surface and material, a deposition produced by various recorders, I-witnesses who've abandoned their sense of self.

I don't want a room of my own; I want a hotel, a caravan. I get off on inversions, reversibility, chiasmus—a word I never knew how to pronounce until I'd heard it spoken to me during a conversation about my work. I want to harness my accidents; I am moved by the glitches that get passed on, mondegreens, defects as defection, exophoric froth. The preliminary should be taken seriously, for its liminal properties, its surrender to trial and especially, to error. An aspiration to be undone. I'm more interested in the other texts—a baker's dozen—hinted, referenced, alluded to or eluded (elided)

---

† As I write this, I am picturing the white headscarves imprinted on the coral tiles, curving a circle around Plaza de Mayo, and all the mothers who walked here, who are still walking, to honor their disappeared children.

across this book, than the text proper. I get off on impropriety.

And anyway, is it or isn't it true that there are so many kinds of surface?—screen, skin, sediment, horizon, exoskeleton, and this mask that I can and cannot simply so simply *take off*.

(I like to turn my screen to dark for five seconds, six. So that attendees can fill in whatever went on in that opaque space, in that unfilmed laboratory of pleasure.)

(Before the period of the sentence contains everything.)

For instance, this aggressive indentation was the result of the way the words looked when I was reading them on my cell phone, when I was writing them down. The point is to encourage the accidental, to invite intrusions, to record everything, everything but everything. And then to play it back.

So Henry James and Gertrude Stein became a pretext or pre-text. To talk about anything, anything else, that was happening or would happen to me. And how I could write myself in, in a way that I never could before.

(I have no patience. But I have so much hope.)

What happens when I have a book published is I read it over and over and over again, until I am reading it as someone reading it instead of as someone who wrote it, someone who is still writing it. As I wrote this note but before I could announce it, L turned to me (we were sitting by a swimming pool; I had a can of beer balanced

in my lap and my phone in my left hand; the sun was drifting in
and out, in and out, the way I like everything) to ask how many
times I'd read the book she was holding in her hand.

(The city was known for its sunrises.)

Basically I am giving you the unprocessed footage. But I am also
giving it to myself, as I try to make sense of it, as I play the reel
back, as I record entangled realities.

In another version of this text, this page has been replaced by a full-
length portrait of Papa John (otherwise known as John Schnatter),
face gleaming with olive oil or sweat, top teeth barely visible (is he
smiling?), what resembles saliva dribbling down his chin, toward
the neck half-held in shadow; the vibrant red uniform of a pizza
purveyor. The caption reads—but it's not important. What's important, or what seems important to me, is the face looking back at
Papa John, father of all mediocre bread and cheese. He's framed in
three-quarters, giving off the impression that he's just been named,
that he's just been called, that someone, somewhere, is asking for
his attention.

(C thought that it would be a great name for a font that launches
words across the internet.)

Western fascism as the boomerang of Western colonialism. What
came first—the universal rights of man or the dehumanization
of men and women who did not look like the founders of liberal
humanism? That we were not, in fact, living in a postcolonial

moment, but only in the next phase of colonial encampment. That there is no Western philosophy without epistemic racism, no universalism without a global colonialism embedded at its center.

I wish to skim—to brush up against without seizing—other moments and other movements, acts that are calculated and improvisational, characterized by an aesthetic of want that bodies, in diasporic desire, *wanting out.*

(Montage as ideal form from which to represent trauma: no such thing as the whole picture, only pieces. And a desire to reassemble.)

Remember that since 1982, the US has designated Cuba a "terrorist nation" despite using its soil to routinely engage in war crimes and human rights violations due to a stipulation stemming from Cuba's independence and the ostensible end of US occupation four years later.

Remember that the post 9/11 "war on terror" coincided with the emergence of extraterritorial US detention centers not beholden to constitutional law nor Geneva Conventions. What today is normalized in the East as in the West was established by George W. Bush and upheld by Barack Obama.

Remember how the Ottoman Empire, the celebrated stretch of land where East and West met, became, in the nineteenth century, "the Levant": a project, or projection, of Orientalism by both the French and the British, who, decades earlier, inaugurated their experiments in visual imperialism—subjugation by means of representation—on China and India.

Remember Abounaddara, the anonymous video art collective formed in the wake of the Syrian civil uprising, whose weekly dispatches bear witness to "small stories, about ordinary people," which contradict the tropes of violence and victimhood and resist the impulse of pity: Syria's "first enemy."

Remember that the refugee can only be seen in the West as a body that is fragmented; that it is only when such persons become decimated and defective that Western viewers can begin the task of reassembling them as a branding exercise of charity and compassion.

What has the *post* in *postcolonial* prevented on the political, artistic, and intellectual levels at present?

The repetition of trauma [as]: the residue of the racialized carceral state that continues to proliferate as legal slave labor and refugee generation—within the prisons, asylums, and detention centers of today.

And is it or isn't it true that literature fixes oral traditions, forcing stories to be repeated in one only one version.

(So many encounters with false memories, glitches in transcription. A tendency for information to degrade each time it's passed on.)

I had said that in Cuba migrants were welcome, so long as they were white, so long as they could beautify the nation in the image of the island's northern neighbors, so long as that whiteness could stamp out the sins of Cuba's slave labor, the country with the second-longest tradition of slavery in the Western hemisphere, a practice that continued until 1886. It was not just Cuba; this kind of conditional hospitality happened across Latin America with alarming frequency during the Second World War. Taking their cue from French republicanism, white delegates across the Caribbean and South America reproduced the republic's exclusionary discourses, dissolving African and Indigenous particularities, remaking each nation in the image of its white European colonizers, cast, in turn, in the role of refugee protector, under the guise of humanitarian aid. How often does a heritage of violence and dislocation adorn itself in assimilation?

With the privilege of passing, of appearing and disappearing on command (a magic trick), with smiling and laughter, with a voice modulated for every room, for every audience, for every occasion, without shame, with the desire to mark shame, smiling on the outside (again), with a repetition that I've always felt necessary, an insecurity and an anxiety that I want to feel has been necessary, with an appetite that can alarm others, vampiric, a hunger for form, for all that can be taken in or can it, with judgment, with uncanny expectations (of myself, of others), with the optimism or idealism to always imagine elsewhere, with the impossibility of return, with a sense of where I came from that exists only in pictures I've had to sketch myself, only in stories passed down or held in, the past as secret, history as residue, with the obsession about alternate rhythms, unencountered trajectories, other chronologies I could have lived, people I could have been or am or will become.

The moment in which anticolonial maneuver turns into "political independence" is the moment imagination is too often impoverished by nationalism, racial and ethnic apartheid, and state autocracy, when the catastrophe of the past catches up with the catastrophe of the future.

[prompt as:] self-portrait with & without

Two years after his first public address on racial discrimination as president of the republic, Fidel Castro declared, in 1961, that the age of racism and discrimination was over.

Whereas a rediscovery and celebration of Cuba's African heritage—following the short-lived Afrocubanismo artistic campaign—served as the heart of revolutionary rhetoric in the years following the 26th of July uprising, Black Cubans are today still excluded from positions in highly coveted tourism jobs and lack the same access to higher education and quality housing as their white counterparts.

Where can we locate the ninety-four-mile distance of the United States from Cuba if not in the chasm of guilt experienced by both the gusano (exile; traitor) and the compañero (Cuban countryman; comrade), a stretch that exceeds coordinates both geographic and generational? If *cubanía* can be expressed, in José Esteban Muñoz's words, as "a structure of feeling that supersedes national boundaries and pedagogies," then perhaps we need to think about how guilt—and shame—can be mobilized into a ledger of accountability and an ethics of care: not just for those who were "left behind" on the island (or for those who, alternatively, have not or can never return) but especially for the Black Cubans in Cuba and abroad who remain alternatively silenced and fetishized, for a Blackness that continues to be obscured in popular national discourses and inter-national ethnic designations, the coalition of pan-Latinx politics that aspires toward a future of inclusion just as it forgets its history of racialization and enslavement.

Unity at the expense of multiplicity—the obliteration of singularity and shared difference as an extant ethnonational project—has its own rich history. Remember Hannah Arendt, and her analysis of inequality through organization in *The Origin of Totalitarianism*:

> The reason why highly developed political communities, such as the ancient city-states or modern nation-states, so often insist on ethnic homogeneity is that they hope to eliminate as far as possible those natural and always present differences and differentiations which by themselves arouse dumb hatred, mistrust, and discrimination because they indicate all too clearly those spheres where men cannot act and change at will.

And yet, is it not also adaptation, and the ability to act on this revision, to alter the present so as to evade a recurrent past, that provides the staging ground for telling one's story?

It is also true that questioning one's own identity, and asking who one wants to become, assumes a certain privilege that precedes the investigation itself. So many others do not have the choice, or rather, the choice is taken from them. Identity, in this scenario, is not to be taken for granted, it is not to be maintained effortlessly, it is not to go uncontested. Identity is the very thing that is demanded of us, the very thing that makes demands on us, on our body, on our body's mobility or the impossibility of it.

At present (a week from now, two months from now, a year), global coloniality is enforced through the governing powers of the United States, through the International Monetary Fund, through the World Bank, through the Pentagon, and through NATO, and moreover, or perhaps more insidiously, through cultural and educational institutions, through humanitarian NGOs, through a world literature that, not unlike the world-system, takes the world as a unit of analysis, yet relegates its thought from a particular perspective.

In re-writing Karl Marx in 1950, Aimé Césaire tried to re-write the cartography of liberal humanism, to make good on what the French—the West—had failed to do: "a humanism made to the measure of the world," and to do so through plunging into the depths. "I felt," Césaire said, "that beneath the social being would be found a profound being, over whom all sorts of ancestral layers and alluviums had been deposited."

That's how the French are, a man on the television says. They fuck people to get intelligence.

Big data's dream: to capture the present so that the future can be predicted and history foretold.

The recent EU-funded AI border security apparatus, iBorderCtrl, which integrates "biometric verification, automated deception detection, document authentication, and risk assessment" to help improve, as its website explains, traveler satisfaction, business, and trade, underscores how the continual digitization of the border obscures material legal and ethical frameworks, not the least of which includes the algorithmic analysis of travelers' bodies: our physical features and our emotional, micro-expressive affects.

Informing the anti-Muslim rhetoric behind the ban on burqas in Austria, France, Belgium, and Denmark in 2018 is the still-celebrated idea that nobody should have their face covered in public; that unfaithful point of view: If I can't see you, I should fear you.

How a face could be both password and lock, how a government's insistence for vigilance could require the installation of more than three hundred million cameras in public places across the world's most populous country, how technology not only tracks faces but also a person's gait, their way of moving. How migrants and asylum applicants could be forced to line up, outside, in harsh, often perilous conditions, for interminable periods, for the opportunity to have their data registered, to qualify for aid.

(Prior to surveillance technology, the state relied on paper documentation, on compulsory identification, on public records, on bureaucratic strategies such as taxation.)

National, sexual, racial, and ethnic identity—the basis of the Western, modern individual—as a categorical construction for an alternative politics will always be limited, and these limitations are inscribed in the narrative of the colonial world from which these markers come. An alternate version of this sentence, which I restrain myself from discarding: Can we articulate any form of radical or antisystemic resistance while reverting to the terms and position of a fundamental colonial construction? I want to say that systemic change necessitates first moving beyond one's subject-position and singular experience. To imagine an antisystemic politics and poetics beyond the identitarian model is to imagine a global, migratory culture that is not clothed in Western universalism and disguised as cosmopolitanism; it is to consider how, when we talk of empire and the experiences of minoritized, racialized, and colonized persons, we are also talking about the experience of migration, the breaks both presupposed and instigated by movement, the epistemological impasses posed by persons on the move.

It is not a question of *escaping identity* but putting it to work; to continue to insist upon identity formations that resist the trappings of capitalism, that resist the trap of commodification, of turning ourselves into commodities. Is it or isn't it true that political, social, and cultural coalition requires, at the same time, that we can mobilize collectively *without* denying our individual material realities? To coexist, then, in mutual difference and to celebrate that shared difference even as we critique and disarm the governing powers of differentiation, omission, and ostracism.

What is the difference between modernism and postmodernism, postmodernism and a kleptocracy? If a knowledge can be "by the people and for the people" then the academy has given its people a study of *the other* from the perspective of itself.

An alternate title to this combination could be called *What Oscar Wilde Knew about Japan.*

Modernity's reorientation of *how* we see forces us to confront not only the ways in which new visual technologies affect how we construct racial difference but how racial difference itself is reinscribed within new technologies. Any analysis of media ecology requires unpacking how such technologies are conceived, how they are practiced, how they problematize the performance of equality; ultimately, how they perform the *problem*.

(For those who can't be technologically apprehended, migrants become the hidden face of capitalism in every sense.)

Y/N: fill in the box that most closely matches the answer.

The dichotomous question is generally a "Yes/No" close-ended question for basic validation. The respondents who answer "Yes" and "No" can be bunched together into groups. This will help companies sort them into subgroups.

The task of taxing a population means enrolling its constituents in the archives of the state. Only when a list like this exists can there be the coordinated dehumanization of a people, as when German occupation authorities exploited the extensive registration imposed on Jewish citizens in the Netherlands in order to round these persons up and deport them to death camps. Only when a name is known can there be a list like this.

Capitalism, so often portrayed as commonsensical and without alternatives, revealed to be dysfunctional during global health crisis. Pandemic "solved" not by nationalistic measures but through a solidarity and common care that exceeds borders.

On the day before Florida would set a national one-day record of COVID infections—surpassing every city, state, and country in the world except the United States, Brazil, and India—Disney World reopened to visitors.

(And alongside their quarterly earnings reports, the presidents, and the publishers, and the chancellors of every institution draw up the balance sheet on colonization.)

Remember how the Indigenous people of pre-Cuba ate fistfuls of dirt until they died. Defenseless and unable to fight, they suicided by refusing Spanish occupation, by returning to the earth what the earth had made.

A related question: What is the difference between a resident and a revenue stream, debt and dispossession? To be exploited, first I must be incorporated into the larger system of others who are like and unlike me. Like a vampire, who must be invited into the home, we are no longer asked to be disposable but also to participate in our own annihilation.

Algorithms don't predict the future so much as they enact it. All outcomes thus become a kind of wish fulfillment brought about by the twinning of predictive analytics and public policy implemented as a consequence. To think of the cost of public safety is to imagine all the capital produced by its production, by its continuous reinforcement, and the residual violence on the targeted, surveilled, captured, and detained bodies, the price—authored in data, authorized through network analysis—to protect the public, to administer the "public space." A related question: Who constitutes the public? Another way of asking this is: *Public for whom?*

When asked about the mask worn by all Mexicans, Carlos Fuentes responded by saying that Latin Americans are much more Italian than Spanish; that the capital of Latin America was not Madrid, but Rome. Against the brutal directness of the Spanish, the Latin American character was one of désir de paraître, which could be translated, from the French that Fuentes borrowed from another novelist (pen name: Stendhal), as the *wish to appear*. And to appear, in its earliest fourteenth-century origins, presupposes distance, a state of concealment; when I was learning to write, to become a writer—by working as a model—this was my first lesson: that in order to become visible to others, I would first have to erase myself, I would first have to obscure myself under the garland of spectacle.

Y/N: Does individual freedom require consenting to coordinated forms of compulsory dependence?

"In fact the whole of Japan is a pure invention," Oscar Wilde wrote, in 1889. "There is no such country, there are no such people." In 1889, Europe was captivated by *japonisme*. French Impressionists were fascinated by the imagined Japan of antiquity and tradition, a pre-Western Japan that didn't exist at the turn of the twentieth century, or rather: a pre-Western Japan that *only* existed at the turn of the twentieth century in the West, scattered on teapots and vases and gouaches and prints.

Must we thus also implicate ourselves, all of us who identify this necessity to perform an alterity that constructs our work as "other"—or otherwise "strange," "interesting," and even "exotic"? We are not only written; we, too, write ourselves—not always from our own perspective, but from the perspective of the people in power. In this specific exchange, the difference that exists between writers of color and the white guardians of the literary-art-academy-institution is imagination. They imagine our experience as [if it were] their own. We imagine that our own experience needs to conform to their generic model, in order to confirm it, to make it legitimate. What ensues is another colonial erasure, which gets celebrated as multiculturalism or postcolonialism or transnationalism or world literature, all of these emanating from and systematized by the West.

(At the turn of the twentieth century, Japan was erecting factories and assembling steamships.)

In the past I called it *the fetishization of hybridity as aesthetic asset of internationalization for the cultural market at large.* Years earlier, Kwame Anthony Appiah, writing during the expansion of refugee studies in the early nineties, described *syncretism*, and understood the clamoring for diversity, the genre of the *neotraditional*, and the intensification of aesthetic individualism as a consequence of the international exchange of commodities. In this scenario, the market, desiring such distinctions, absorbs the artist's life into the work itself; modes of identity become "modes of identifying objects."

What does it mean to be denied your own history?

Dream (of another writer's dream) about a rectangular sheet of white paper (a napkin?) given to those about to be executed. I am allowed to write on the thin slip, which is to be placed inside or over my mouth at the moment of execution. Do I die of choking (on language, on my own words) or by the violence that precedes artistic production?

The only people I befriended at ABC Studios, to which I'd travel, walking north from Columbus Circle in the same black jeans, the same white undershirt, facing west (in the direction of the Hudson River; the rush of wind and tourists) each week, twice a week, to perform a diverse set of roles across an array of soaps, were the wardrobe stylists. It took me so many years to understand why. They gave us costumes and we wore them.

What have I inherited but the project of multiculturalism that annihilates each and every difference in its global purview, the Latino/a/x that lacks geographic, racial, and historical specificity? And if s asked me again about why my work is never linked with an Eastern European Studies or Slavic Studies or Polish Studies, or Polish Literature, or *Polish* as indexical cultural marker, I'd tell her to give thanks, to feel thankful, that your place of birth has not turned into an academic keyword, fetishized and at the same time enfeebled, commodified through the project of internationalization that voyages into the periphery, and rescues it from obliteration.

[remember:] the constitution of the subject is inextricable from the enactment of subjugation; the performance of individuation can't or won't come off without the process of normalization, the conformation or confirmation of one's own alleged "usual" or "expected" state or condition

What happens is that the glass is dirty. So when we look at ourselves in the mirror, all we can see is a face marked with dirt that is not our own but that has been given to us; a face that has been designed for us, a voice that is not one we recognize.

The only copies of the two photographs I have of s and j as children are the ones that appear on thin white printing paper, produced from a photograph I'd taken of the physical originals, which have gone missing. In this book, these images of each of my parents have been digitally photographed, then printed out, then scanned back into an electronic copy, then sharpened and reprocessed by an acquaintance, who I met on the internet.[‡] An attempt to remove the noise of mediation, or to heighten it. N said that he wanted to restore the originals. Can a copy of a copy of a copy of a copy become restored to an original? I nevertheless welcomed the invitation, knowing that these photos, like the persons they contain, have migrated elsewhere, lived lives that are multiple.

[‡] Then printed out again, probably. If what we're reading is really a book.

The discovering, he said, began after I moved. Photographing in my day to day, I began filming, using time to figure out how we've come to be seen.

(The screen expands, like before a movie at the cinema.)

I watched a bird lick the frost off the edges of my body in the morning when I was only a single blade of grass, a single gasp of that little bird's delight, and watched as she knelt before me before she

flew away.

He writes poetry and plays in his free time.

I yearn for the smell of a coffee that doesn't belong to me, the sound of another person's music floating below or above, the words themselves, lost and found—the way I pick up everything—conversations about a union meeting and the late-night happy hour on Cortelyou and the appointment at the nail salon and Jackie's cousin's aunt mingling on a single interface, the way the city is the fantasy of the internet before there was the internet. Revealing something to me *on the surface*, and only because every narrative here becomes intertextual. I yearn for the feeling of sliding in, or hunching down, or hoisting myself up, arms over my head to reach the top, the very top of the train car, balancing against the flesh of every other person I'd otherwise never know. Everything written in order or out of order so as to be lived twice, and lived again for the first time. I imagine the history of touch the way I imagine all the history books I ever was forced to thumb through in elementary school: big blocks of dust, telling me that everything that ever began always and already ended. As if history, objective, immovable, was something that could only ever be viewed from its aftermath, something that could only ever be viewed on a flimsy piece of textbook paper: black print adjacent to a shitty stock photo. As if history could only ever be viewed from so many distances, instead of up against it, skin on skin.

I'm a wilted asparagus, overdone, charred at each edge. Some people take me in and smell quite different. I never could tell whether it was a question of recognition or the scent itself. Identified in passing or not at all. I'm a rider, leg over leg, comfortable to be sitting up straight, practicing my posture while moving. A poached egg, exquisite but haphazard, threatening to ruin itself without warning, to spill and be spilled. The butter that laces any good pancake, indispensable but undetectable. Meaning that can only be gleaned through reading one's own lips.

The holy trinity, my classmates said, when I showed them one of the two copies. The holy trinity? I asked. Three daughters; three children. Then there were four. A boy named Kazimierz, which was shortened to Kaziu, and later to Kaz, at least by the time I was born. K and S and H and J and I and all of them lived upstairs from a funeral parlor in Greenpoint after arriving in the United States. They lived like ghosts. But also: they lived with ghosts.

She was watching from the window, arms out, hanging from the ledge reaching toward me—your uncle was still an infant—and when she stepped inside I saw that I could see right through her. That was the first time. I saw her again, the same position, clutching air in each arm, cradling space. Another night I woke to find a man, bald and mustached, suspended inside the wall. He looked like he was choking. I recalled a boy, his face against the wooden floor, a sound like marbles dropping when he'd bang his head throughout the hours I lay awake, too mindful to shut my eyes. We lived on water, we lived on spoiled rice cooked slow, stirred even slower, we lived on cabbage, couldn't hardly make kapusta, gołąbki, couldn't hardly get milk unless it was postdated, unless we waited that long. We gathered change on the street, we huddled close and bathed fast. We kept on

(A feeling like falling in space, on the edge of it, up against it, eyes closed.)

seeing strangers, every evening. We were never lonely, counting the hours—the before and the after touch, trembling along the walls. I thought I'd never leave Brooklyn, I thought I'd never be anyone but the girl in slip-ons and gray stockings on a stoop on Diamond Street. So many afternoons I watched the windows. Hungry all the time, I watched the people inside, wanting whatever it was they ate or owned. Imagining I could be like anyone else in America.

In the photograph, my mom is the one who is crying.

I want to itemize and order *thoughts as they occur* to me, knowing that what's here begs what's missing. In that unknowability I want to remember or remind myself that the aspiration of every book is to make a world, and to make a world requires accumulating things but also losing them, the way content picks up information and also drops it, as it carries or is carried toward some uncertain present.

The previous video segment was two minutes and twelve seconds long.

Never registered the shame of a wet dream. Conversely, remember often wanting to access such a dream, such an experience, in all its unconscious wetness. Would relish any opportunity to arise, into the joy of another day, encased in sheets that were suffused with my insides; evidence of involuntary pleasure, which seems to me to be the greatest kind.

(A certain euphoria arises in response to the inadvertent and uncontrollable.)

The name of the popular beautifying app Facetune suggests that the face is a rhythmic composition, but also an instrument for playing, a utensil for uncorrected pleasure.

Staging failure offers us a new way to think about the conditions of contemporary communication and the exploitation of information and optic systems within our current migratory drift, wherein biometric practices are enforced at border control checkpoints, asylum application interviews, admittance to refugee shelters, residence and naturalization processes, and evaluations of eligibility for basic human rights, like education and healthcare.[§]

---

§ The process of applying documentation with images to track and control individual citizens and migrants was devised, not coincidentally, by a French police officer, Alphonse Bertillon, who standardized the practice of applying anthropological technique to law enforcement in Paris at the end of the nineteenth century.

If 1989 saw the collapse of the Berlin Wall and the diffusion of democracy across Europe, then two years later, the Strait of Gibraltar became another border, a perilous, suffocating, one-way route for people—some separated only by nine miles—who could no longer travel freely to fortress Europe.

That's who we are. The face which hides itself so it can be shown. The name that keeps quiet in order to be named. Behind our unspeakable name. Behind the we that you see. Behind us we are (at) you.

I've asked us to think more often in the future perfect. What will we have been? Understanding that being so often necessitates doing and doing necessitates a way of being in the world: the reinvention of space. If asked to suggest a genre for this book I would say a *mobility*.

What is at stake is not just the ability to pass, but the possibilities and attendant challenges of redistributing power and agency within sites of cross-cultural exchange, informing extant issues of privacy but also raising questions about public space.

Systemic change requires true coalition, but it also means addressing the ways in which our movements—whether they are situated in immigrants' rights, women's rights, workers' rights, LGBT+ rights, or any other—have advanced racist, ableist, heteronormative, cisgender, and nationalist frameworks in the name of equality.

Such is the move from undesirable body parts to undesirable bodies within a digital democracy that exploits the uneven distribution of digital technology, occasions in which noise is indeed separated from signal, not to render successful transmission, but to exclude specific receivers, disposing of political and social rights as a literal manner of form.

Might we take the herraguas of Morocco and its neighboring countries at their word? Since the early nineties, these "burners," unable to apply for an inordinately expensive visa produced through the Schengen Agreement, and unwilling to submit to its application's required biometric scan, have abandoned their own signification as citizens within a national polity and as migrants within a human rights regime that will attempt to sort them upon arrival by setting their identity documents ablaze. In critiquing a normative and exclusionary national citizenship as well as the supranational entities that manage the flow of capital and persons, the herragua becomes neither subject nor object; stripped of the Western markers of the consumer/commodity individual subject, they become no longer legible except as humans.

In conceptualizing a mobile commons and a migrant sovereignty premised on documentation, self-forgery, countersurveillance, and anonymity, it becomes imperative to parse the distinctions between *effacement* and *erasure*. In this project, what is the final reformulation of space and self?

The migrant who refuses to consent to the national discourses of migration and the international framework of refugee (the narrative tropes of the [un]deserving migrant), the migrant who refuses to participate in the construction of their own debasement or celebration, is not erasing their material experience as a person displaced, exiled, or in transit, but in fact returning it to the public as a political inquiry: a critique of the system of collection, categorization, supervision, documentation, and assimilation that colludes to keep them in place. In this context, effacement becomes a visible mark, the stroke of redaction or remediation that is also a blur, and a blur that signifies the tempo of an attempted mobility.

Remember the magic marker, which erases as it overlaps ink. Remember the importance of transcription, a trace but also an omen, every stroke as a sigil. To efface is not to erase because what is made clear by such marks is the processes by which a person might return themselves to autonomy, a heightened transparency made possible only through the repetition of effacement, and the imbrication of selves and artistic forms from which to re-present the individual as unnamed collective. To respond to the either/or of repatriation and naturalization is thus to be visible as something other than migrant-refugee or national citizen-subject; to efface *one's self as such* is to enact different modes of identity, which is to say different modes of appearance and presence: a different representation of community.

I am jealous, whenever I hear about another friend's earliest memories. They were always so much earlier, so much more primal than my own. In my life (at least how I'm remembering it), memory began with words, with a certain kind of recognition, which was reading. I remember nothing before I learned to read. My past began in books. And so I often wonder whether my life has been fictionalized for far longer than the moment I decided to write about it.

"Dreaming has a share in history," Walter Benjamin writes. What is forgotten, I think, is that history, too, must have a share in dreams. And what I mean is that what remains to be written is not the history of the dream, as Benjamin argued, but the dream of history. That history can be re-written through dreams, the residue of our subconscious that alters the trajectory of our waking, conscious life.

(Trauma of exile as a dream that keeps repeating.)

Asylum as invitation: for the nation to be absolved of its past through reproducing the script of liberal progressiveness and liberating savior, reenacting the scene of rescue (the scene of violence) of the "developing world"

In the waning days of 2020, when Singapore was preparing for its final phase of reopening, its low-wage migrant workers—who had accounted for 93 percent of the city-state's official COVID cases—remained confined to dormitories, barred from leaving their buildings under government lockdown. The majority of the workers—persons responsible for their host republic's ability to persist in a constant state of construction (renovation, modernization), building the infrastructures of Singapore's neoliberal economy—had come from India and Bangladesh, impoverished rural regions that the island has historically relied upon for labor.

The Singaporean government, which separates its virus-infection statistics into two categories—one for migrant workers and one for "the community"—has periodically allowed its migrant workers to apply for permission for three-hour visits to designated "recreation centers," where they can contribute to the economy in other ways (by shopping). Some workers, according to the Ministry of Health, will eventually be rewarded once-a-month access to "the community," an eligibility contingent upon compulsory surveillance.

I want to think about how memory might serve, not as a monument to the past, but as an instrument that informs our capacity to analyze the present. Memory, from Latin *memoria*: mindful, connected to Late Latin *martyr*: witness, related to the Greek *mermēra*: care.

To be mindful is to be aware, to attend to, to devote attention and concern, to *keep* a thing or person *in mind*.

If there is a truth, we have had to invent it. The digressions, the gaps, the mistranslations, the silences serve as a reminder that movement does not have to be tied to tragedy; that movement need not be directed by the either/or of flight and return. In returning to the question of identity, to what characterizes a shared Latin heritage, or Latinidad, Juana María Rodríguez moves beyond language—beyond the imposed and Indigenous languages spoken in Latin America and the Caribbean and to the shared legacy of colonization. "Spain and Portugal also spread their colonial seeds everywhere," Rodríguez writes, "in the Philippines, the Canary Islands, Cape Verde, Morocco, Macao, Mozambique, Guinea Bissau, and Angola, for example. In México, the mixture of Indigenous and Spanish blood is considered *mestizo*, yet in the Philippines this same mixture is considered Asian." What are the ways in which our imposed and asserted identities work in tandem to undermine a shared politics, by obfuscating the various political projects in which these identity positions are grounded? What is at stake is legibility; the conflation of race, ethnicity, nation, culture; the reproduction of assimilation to an imaginary whole. How simulation entangles that. How simulation seeks neither completion nor preservation but dis-integration.

(One or more of the message components have been deleted by MMS Adaptation. Either the message was too large, or the components were unsuitable for your handset.)

I think again of my abuelo, J, like my brother, like my dad, like no one but himself, "El Chino," and how maybe his familiar and familial nickname served another point, an unintended or unintentional gesture toward our heritage of colonization and displacement and ultimately, dispersion. The transnational imagination demands that we read the names and categories by which we are hailed and which we ourselves employ as both less and more than what they pretend to portray.

Faces on Facetune look plastic and flat, as if heavy cream was lathered on top of skin, shredded of all contour, all expressive movement, all emotion—not even the eyes, lit like ersatz jewels under a pawn lamp, left intact. Static, the face yet trembles, as if the person I am looking at, the person looking at me, is wearing a mold instead of a face.

(We are the aliens that we dreamt of.)

If we believe that "liminality" and "hybridity" are necessary characteristics of the colonial subject, as Homi Bhabha suggests, then I would like to imagine Cuba as an ideal setting for *transculturación* to flourish: a memory, or remainder, of the multiple and various colonizations of the Caribbean, the multiple and various colonizations of the Americas. The cracks in colonial discourse are this hybridity: the failure—the impossibility—of the colonial system to reproduce itself fully.

Information across the artist's website is frequently redacted, including the homepage's succession of questionnaires, each one containing biographical data about other people. One could write a book about the artist's uses of dissimulation, self-forgery, and a scrapbook aesthetic, and how it responds to the unrepresentable events of _____ and the offices of "official truth": their production of the production of history. This is not that book.

That *limen* can be both threshold (Latin) and also refuge (Greek), if we go far enough, if we go deep enough, if we recover more than just etymology but especially everything that words harbor outside a recorded historical development; that liminality enacts a boundary moment *and* the ability to move into that momentary space. Any discussion of a celebrated "hybrid poetics" or "liminal poetics" (or similarly fashionable "border poetics") begs closer attention to passage and its rites.

At the roller rink, a strobe shoots through the moving bodies, so that glances become more than moments of apprehension but interviews in the dark against the backdrop of confetti, and the sound of plastic ricocheting off something by Technotronic, something by

Real McCoy and La Bouche and, if there's a glitch in the memory, Tommy Genesis. Forgetting what was dusk, what was dawn. I am five in this scene. I've just turned five or I'll turn five in a moment more. I love spinning around and around and around, arms up, a thin tube of neon green glowing around my neck until I fall in love. In the dark, I remember mouthing, to no one but myself, everyone looks like everyone else.

What do we shed after language but earth?

(When s wanted to clean my dirty mouth, she'd press a bar of Irish Spring there. And before that—the warnings, a threat: I'm going to have to wash your mouth out with soap.)

In this correspondence, every letter as a sound-image-object bears divine messages.

Juan was later John, just as Zosia became Sophie, as if my parents, by changing their names, could also change the memories they carried from home. As if when z became s, the intent was also to reemerge as the other. Maybe the transliteration of J becoming J smuggled in a parable about the impossibility of the task: no transformation is ever total; no disappearance is ever absolute.

Perhaps, I wrote, I had always been searching for my double.

Stuart Hall, in his analysis and interrogation of "multiculturalism" within contemporary British society and political discourse, considers hybridity as "another term for the cultural logic of *translation* . . . which is agonistic because it is never completed." If hybridity can be read as a translation, then I want to elaborate this process of identity formation as a collaborative act—a rendering that is always multiple, unequal, open-ended—to understand how incompletion might productively undo the particular and the universal as vocabularies of society, no longer faced with the choice between the artificial homogeneity of the nation or the inflated difference of their past, the latter too often coded in racial and ethnic terms. What hybridity as translation (translation as hybridity) asserts is exactly this lack, a wish to assume a sense of self—and belonging—absent the binary alignment of nation, in which hyphens confirm rather than contest and negotiate difference.

We saw each other—we passed glances, we gave and were given back [to] ourselves—in the length of a film frame.

(Desire to become myself a *magic marker*; to advance through erasure, or articulate a mobility premised on disappearance.)

The mirror is a zone of intensity. Skin moves across surface, is deformed, penetrated, resurfaces as a thought, which passes in the interval between glimpse and appraisal. Between a face and its turning away. I want to think of my face when it is already turned away from its likeness, which is me.

(In this way I become, like my characters, a variable; or: I receive a variation of myself.)

My task is to re-create what the eye sees at certain angles, at certain intervals. (And underlined, below this:) The book as a series of evaporating glances?

A few weeks after I was born, *Gotcha!* debuted in theaters across the United States. In the film, a shy UCLA veterinary student and the reigning champion at "Gotcha," a campus-wide paintball game, gets seduced by an older woman while on vacation in West Germany. The woman turns out to be an international spy. The shy UCLA veterinary student unwittingly becomes an accomplice, transporting a package he thinks contains a strudel, from East Germany back into West Germany, crossing via Checkpoint Charlie, and eventually, escaping from the Soviets with the help of a German rock band headed for Hamburg, who offers him a ride to the airport.

I want to know what was in the strudel, if it was a strudel. Apple or cherry? Or something more peculiar?

When I am distracted, when I am looking for a long time and at nothing, when I am forgetful or forgetting, when I am blank with expectation and concern, when I am emptied of all meaning, I am most myself. These moments happen most often when I move, as I am moving, in the moment of movement or when movement has stalled, however briefly. When movement has stalled, it's so often to allow others to get on, or get in.

When he returns home to Los Angeles, there is a strange canister of film in his backpack and a team of KGB agents on his back. Suddenly he is in the middle of a real life-or-death game of "Gotcha."

Height of narcissism, or the condition of writing, of the writer: to imagine that everyone who populates the landscape need only to be looked at to appear, or more accurately: to reappear. (This gaze includes the writer, who is also a character come to life.)

She's one of those movie talents who seem to materialize out of thin air, a genuine original, Roger Ebert wrote, of Linda Fiorentino, who plays Sasha, the Czechoslovakian spy. This is her second movie; her first was *Vision Quest*, where she played the drifter who wandered into Matthew Modine's life and encouraged his quest for a state wrestling championship.

(I don't write plots; I only remember them.)

The future of mobility is at stake in any vision of a post-pandemic worldview, and it will have to involve questions that require us to think not only about the displacement and forced migration that follows climate change as well as military and economic violence, but also the internal exclusion and systemic inequalities brought about by our political and social structures, the unequal access that citizenship elides.

Image may contain: 1 person, smiling, text
Image may contain: 1 person, close up
Image may contain: night, sky, and outdoor
Image may contain: 1 or more people, people sitting, shoes, and indoor

The ceremony of naturalization has been described, in the United States as elsewhere, as a "rite of passage." What passes is not the individual, who is now neither a foreigner nor naturally—by birth—a citizen, but the *pastimes* of the nation, in which exclusion and inclusion are intermingled and mutually constitutive.

Even before shelter-in-place orders, the rise of nationalism in the Americas and throughout Europe—alongside normalized racism, right-wing immigration policies, anti-globalism discourse, and increasing practices of securitization—had already cast a threatening cloud over the future of mobility. Politicians across the European Union began to exploit the virus by directing blame at migrants, targeting specific nationalities on the pretext of containing the spread of disease. The President of the United States said that he intended to suspend all immigration to the country. Closing our borders, he recites, as he strains his eyes, reading from a teleprompter, will protect American workers once the economy reopens. In Mexico's northern border cities, as nonessential businesses closed and manufacturing halted across the world, work in US-owned factories continued; a month later, these maquiladoras became loci of outbreaks.

(In the global market, the value of a human life continues its downswing.)

And hardly any body today remains unsigned-for, and it isn't just our bodies, but our minds. Biometric technologies "of intent" use cognitive sciences and neurobehavioral queues in screening processes, scanning and measuring emotional valences to help safeguard the nation from outside threats.

Unlike the past, when an objectified body could return that look, recycle the interpellating gaze; when an objectified body could, in effect, object to their own abjection by another, today we are being hailed by biometric technologies, we are being surveilled and sorted, we are being identified and interpreted as data.

There is no possibility to *look back.*

And still the unavoidable urge to trace, or at least to flesh out a genealogy without origin. What is the avant-garde, and what are the properties by which we measure it?—political, aesthetic, theoretical? Can the avant-garde (co)exist with(in) the academy or the institution? Or is the avant-garde marked by its opposition to both the institution and mass culture? Instead of being propelled by prescriptive conditions, can the relationship between the "avant-garde" and other cultures be dialectical (as opposed to oppositional)?

A related question: To what extent does a queer aesthetics operate within and without the institution as a working in and against, and even more: working near other discourses (such as feminism, hybridity, diaspora, deconstruction, decoloniality, etc.)? I want to invite, to continue to invite an aesthetics of attraction, which is about nearness but also about similitude (doubles, correspondences, resemblances). *Like:* to welcome other discourses/traditions/methodologies/technologies as a queer aesthetic (so as to work with them and work on them).

Minus the constant financial struggle, there is also the recurring theme of loneliness.

And when I sign my name, I only double my first initial.

A *certified copy* is a copy (often a photocopy) of a primary document that has on it an endorsement or certificate that it is a true copy of the primary document. It does not certify that the primary document is genuine, only that it is a true copy of the primary document. The certified copy is signed by a person nominated by the person or agency asking for it. Typically, the person is referred to as an *authorized person*. The person who is authorized to sign the certificate will vary between countries.

When we play this back, we take the sound off. Muted, it makes each viewer feel as if they are looking in on a dream.

Pero mientras sea desaparecido, no puede tener ningún tratamiento especial, es una incognita, es un desaparecido, no tiene entidad, no está, ni muerto ni vivo, está desaparecido.

In a press conference in 1979, Jorge Rafael Videla, dictator of Argentina between 1976 and 1981, said exactly that.

What does it mean to be un desaparecido? To not have any entity; to be neither dead nor alive.

What does it mean to be permanently *missing*?

(*Traum*, in German, is "dream.")

"We sublimated in art what we weren't allowed to live in life."

The flip side of a postindustrial consumer economy is an economy of waste. How does trash saturation inform a broader culture of global precarity? Capitalism mimics itself through its own conquest, an iteration toward a desired result, which ends in refuse and refusal: material waste and wasted humans.

(Like Peter Fitzek's angel currency, this book has an elusive relationship to value.)

It is this, only this: unprotected screen on screen action, where I am alone, along with others, also alone, to be looking at and on, to be looking over—a lecture, a chapter, a budget, an overview of *events we wish to plan in the future.*

(I want to be serious, and I want to have fun doing it.)

The book as an arena for testing out ideas and theories, for foraging and also forging stories.

I write words by clicking, photographing sensations as I alight upon them in my viewfinder, a useful tool and a preexisting condition—not illness or injury but endowment—I've always thought, of any writer.

(As soon as I photograph myself, my dataset evolves into something incrementally more countable and categorizable, searchable and thus surveillable.)

> how solid how solid
> big bellies can be

E presents his followers with his lunch, photographed every

afternoon for the last seventy-three days. I begin typing a comment; I hit *post*. You could say that your tuna sandwich is watching you just as much as you are gazing longingly at it; the question is only who blinks first. You could say that the commodity fetish not only speaks in 2020; it speaks our name.

[market empire/market emperors:] they had the idea that the reassembly of the *local* into accessible iterations could also invent *authenticity*

& to conjure the authentic is also to construct its opposite: the foreign

Since 1983, the Ejército Zapatista de Liberación Nacional has advanced what has come to be known as alter-globalization (or alter-mundialization), an anti-neoliberal social movement that supports global cooperation and interaction, while opposing economic globalization. The Zapatistas champion environmental and climate protection, economic justice, civil liberties, and the protection of Indigenous cultures and land. The group, which has no official leader, went public on the first day of 1994, its declaration coinciding with the establishment of the North American Free Trade Agreement.

G writes to me, and his messages appear with a sound, a notification of instantaneous arrival. Things have been going very well here, thankfully. We have to a great extent "beaten" the infection curve. I love, G writes, that the expression used in Mexico at the moment is "domar la curva."

On that day, they issued their First Declaration and Revolutionary Laws from the Lacandon Jungle, an area of rainforest that stretches from Chiapas, Mexico, into Honduras, and across the southern part of the Yucatán Peninsula.

Waiting, like writing, is a bodily exercise. I constrict and I tighten. I elongate and spread my thighs as I lean over, as I beg the text to come closer.

Naturalization as the enforcement of difference through the performance of equality, a ritual of request and approval that affirms the sovereignty of the state by recalling the identity of the nation.

It is no coincidence that the rising number of new French citizens via naturalization after September 11, 2001, occurs at the very moment France imposes tighter reins on immigration.

(Remember to look for corresponding data within the United States; remember to interrogate the twinning of *illegality* and *ceremony*, the ways in which nations restrict the influx of persons at the same time that they rid their own population of "foreigners.")

Some people (sometimes I can convince myself of this) know everything they want to write before they write it down. I am not of that ilk, preferring not to know even the direction of the sentence as it is being written. And what joy to find my fingers on a letter, a series of graphs or characters, which had gone unnoticed until now.

What happens when we become the thing we set out to overcome?

I take into account my own positionality as a postcolonial subject. I do not mean that I am done with it. No, he said, I'm not done with it. I am infected by it.

Common Zapatista saying: "luchar por un mundo donde otros mundos sean posibles."

P wants to know what I'm writing, what it is I'm writing now. I tell P I'm writing a dictionary. Because when I was young, I used to read the dictionary like it was a book of literature. And the sense of discovery, the urgency of a new word coming into breath or being, a new mode of thinking, an activity, which was a game—all of this still returns to me whenever I re-read the dictionary, whenever I look up from a book.

Fight for a world where *other worlds are possible*.

I want to break off a word or line, as if it were a branch, and the text were a tree. And then I'd want to repeat that word or line at various moments throughout the text, as if I were trying to produce another tree, a second, a third, from the outside in, instead of from deep, deep under the earth. Can writing be a form of gardening, in reverse? As if each tree, even if it resembles the ones around it, has a different voice. And then I want to listen for the discrepancies.

(A certain dedication in the lips, the roving mouth.)

Who or what is being heard, or misheard? And how do these inter-ferences produce meaning through being played (as if overlaying a sample on an audio track)? Who was it who was it who told me the moment we have to accept an unnoticed detail is the moment we dominate it?

In Spanish, "domar" is to overcome, to break or break in, to bring (under the control of), to get (in line), to curb or restrain, to check, to tame.

I've thought often about my desires, about my specific desire to take my lover in from behind, and how my lover helps by reaching back, by gliding one hand, and how my lover pants and pushes their body closer to mine, so that we may merge deeper, and how my eyes drop, or seem to, behind each lid when I let my palms drop to my thighs, bent down, with our knees nearly touching, and how this release comes only after an experience of domination, and a domination that is the permission to *take over*. How my desire to take my lover in from behind (and to know that where there is desire there is fear) relies on these power dynamics; an awareness of control; to see without having all the time to be seen. How I am not so different, then, from all the people and things I scorn, the people and things I resist, the ideologies and programs I renounce, the History I disavow. And then I wonder, what does that make me? I wonder: what does that make me then?

we the people

The photograph predates the memory, which doesn't exist. Since I was three years old, or maybe four. It must have been 1989, or 1990, because the palm fronds are nearly neon green, the midday sun a shade of orange, pink, and bright yellow. My reflected ghost from the future intervening, or interrogating, the printed surface that I've photographed again—confusing one copy for another—bringing the past closer or else relating the distance, such that my doughy toddler arms and the rectangular device held against my chest might all be seen as another segment of the fibrous palm tree, which holds half my face, the three-year-old face, three and a half years going on four, in shadow.

I am holding a bottle of beer, so small its sepia barrel barely reaches beyond my open hand. The person behind the camera, probably my dad, took the photo after he'd placed the bottle in my hands, and because he'd placed the bottle in my hands. Baby and his bottle. That's what the caption says, written in cursive blue ink on the back of the resin coated paper image, if you've taken it out of its plastic sheet, flipped it around in your own hand. The bottle didn't have any beer in it, at least not the kind many people might expect. It was a Malta, the non-alcoholic Cuban cola brewed with molasses, barley, and hops, whose faint carbonation was my early entry point into soda pop, the thrill of carrying bubbles on the tongue, unless the thrill came from the risk of their abrupt dispersal. Look closer. The man on the bottle, his hair in a bun, his ears wreathed in ringlets, is framed in portrait, in profile, his eyes cast toward the viewer's left, if you're holding the front of the bottle as you look at it. Look again. His head lunges forward; the neck kneels in deference or out of some uncertain strain; the nape rims the bottle's alphabetical insignia, above which the image ends, making way for the oblong *U* that I confused, for many years after, with a *V*, a brand that shares its name with a town in Cuba, itself an homage to the Taíno chief who was burned there, at the stake, by the Spaniards. A Taíno chief who, after departing the Hispaniola province of Guahaba (present-day Haiti) by canoe to warn the Indigenous people of Cuba about the conquistadores' imminent arrival, initiated a pan-Caribbean resistance, mobilized enslaved Africans and Indigenous tribes, was captured and interrogated, refused conversion to Christianity, requested to go to Hell, since Hell, as it was confirmed to him by the Franciscan friar that provided his last rites, was a place absent the Spanish, on account of their devout faith, their supreme piety.¶ Flip the photograph back, so that my half-open eyes are again facing yours. Your own eyes, looking back. The fluttering eyelids like curtains, swaying above a stage.

How did a Taíno chief end up on this bottle of beer? Which is to say: Why?

Hatuey, in profile, is turning his gaze north, turning his gaze west. From Haiti, he leans, throat jutted, scanning the sea that separates him from Cuba's eastern coast, knowing what he will do in spite of everything that has already occurred, and why, which is progress, the eradication of the present. He is looking, not to the future, but to the past.

¶ The priest tells us: In memory of Christ and the Twelve Apostles, the Spanish forces would hang Taínos in groups of thirteen before burning them alive.

My bottle of Malta Hatuey isn't an álbum de vistas—the popular genre of viewing albums that dominated the European imaginary of the earth's Western Hemisphere from the sixteenth century all the way through the turn of the twentieth, when photographs replaced copper engravings and wood-cut etchings—but it can be read as an extant artifact of the state's implementation of scopic recognition to rationalize the subjugation of persons contained within a frame and ventriloquized by captions, a verbal-visual exhibit in miniature, in which the shift from imagined to exterminated bodies became, for the Latin American governments that employed them in pursuit of the production of nation, merely a matter of form.

Legalized slavery may have finally ended in Cuba on October 7, 1886, but the complex assemblage of surveillance, travel narrative, documentary, and portraiture to fortify an unbroken chain of mass eviction—by death or deportation—economic exploitation, and white supremacy continues without interruption. Remember the Castro regime's implementation of the film camera as a utensil for socialist realism, the photographic image as a unit of naturalized reality in the realm of art as in life; remember the link between the wholesale usurpation of what can be counted, that is registered, as real, and the policies of totalitarianism. The history of resistance in the realms of politics and pedagogy and art reminds us that what may be concretized on the level of material action must first be imagined. But it works just the same for the predominant powers, a rehearsal of visual imperialism that exceeds the theater of Latin America.

Remember that to be seen is also to be looked at, exposed, and thus brought to light, kindled, convertible: the etymological death mask of any "image" mounted in the word's Latin origins. I often wonder about the consequences of visibility; a culture of enforced outing, or the metrics of identification and recognition, of *being out*, against which non-legibility—non-visibility—is equivalent to humankind's passing into disposability; the upshot of representation when the image, circulated and celebrated, begins to replace the real. And the residue, too, of a revolution premised on the independence and equality of its most vulnerable citizens in a nation with the second-longest history of slavery, a revolutionary regime which, nevertheless, reproduced the racial violence of the republics it replaced.

"Patria o muerte, venceremos," so said Fidel Castro months after Fulgencio Batista was ousted, during a memorial for dead workers, glorified victims, in March of 1960. Homeland or death, we will prevail. Who is the *we* of Cuba's national motto? Decades later, during the initial outbreak of COVID-19 and the all-day demonstrations in the city of my father's birth protesting the policies and practices of newly appointed First Secretary Miguel Díaz-Canel, *Patria y Vida* became another rallying call for the Cuban people, who had to invert postrevolutionary rhetoric in order to reconsider its failed promises. Homeland and life.

An alternate title to this combination could be called *Che Guevara's collection of Rolexes.*

"But before the white man," Guillermo Cabrera Infante writes of his native Cuba, "were the Indians. The first to arrive—they came, like all of them, from the continent—were the Ciboneys. Then came the Taínos, who treated the Ciboneys like servants. . . . In turn the Taínos and the Ciboneys were at the mercy of the Caribs . . . the Caribs were fierce and proud and had a motto: *'Ana carina roto'*—'Only we are people.'"

But before Hatuey turned up here, in my outstretched hands on my bottle of Malta, on this lithographed portrait framed in profile, in this photograph that predates memory, he was a martyr. The first hero of Cuba, they say, except he was burned to make Cuba what it is and what it would become.

Only we are people. Only we are people. Only we are people. Only we are people. Only we are people. We the people. We the people. We the people of the United States. Without a pause, without a comma. Order . . . Union . . . Justice . . . domestic Tranquility . . . the common defense . . . the general Welfare . . . and secure the Blessings of Liberty to ourselves and our Posterity. Since only we are people. We the people. United. The Carib's motto, terrifying in its calm calculations, merges with the Preamble to the US Constitution; a new verse shrieks between my ears, and I can't rewind; I cannot turn my gaze or forget how it is I arrived here, with you. When my neighbors ask what it is I'm working on all day and into the night, I tell them a rough translation of *North by Northwest*, by which I mean a movie, a series of film strips, or the scrapbook through which they continue to be inserted, and recombined. This is why the arrangement of the album is just as important as the white space that surrounds each visual-verbal inscription. I am interested in what the images cannot say.

matt damon's resemblance

(a sonata)

In Marseilles, while waiting to be asked what it is I would like, what I want, I came across a person, a stranger, to whom I dedicate this sequence.

What is the difference between remembering and repeating?

In an essay, w stands mesmerized (though in the past tense), clicking on a touchscreen that says, "click me." Obedient and astounded, he repeats the gesture, not in spite of the fact that nothing happens, but maybe (I think) *because* nothing happens. I kept doing it, w writes, and I enjoyed the experience . . .

We were sitting across from each other in an alleyway that had been refashioned into a restaurant's dining room. I had walked in, climbing the steps, the curving hill from Le Vieux Port; I had come across this person, who was already seated, who had already been sitting, whose face I can and cannot remember. The best faces, or the faces I'm most attracted to, I often think, are the faces that solicit recognition but also haze. And it is with this same faithful and unfastened glance that I sketch their face now: the head tilted, slightly, leaning back, the hair slipping over one eye—the left—the right hand—their palm—folded on the lap; a yacht, or sailboat (I can't tell the difference) moving into their vantage point (mine was facing a red-bricked wall), a smooth traversal, I imagined, but not silent.

(Originally, this scene occurred in Paris, on the Paris Metro, as I, riding the pink line, allowed myself the pleasure of delaying an ultimate destination.)

remember: to resist prose's
capacity to run cold

We got off at Pont Neuf; I had intended to ride the pink line all the way to Gare du Nord (unconnectable) because I had to be somewhere else in France, and I was already a day late. We looked at each other—we'd stood up, together, when the doors slid open—and exited without words, reemerging into the city, where it had just rained, where it had just been raining, where rain (or its remainder) slid down my hair, to my forehead—a part of my face I can never remember or that is not worth mentioning—as we entered a café. What did we drink, or did we only sit, in place, across from each other, as if we were still riding the pink line, the only movement the movement of pedestrians outside, congregating around the Seine, all those persons passing who, I sometimes feel, I felt that day, were passing for us. When they returned from the toilet, I stood up and traced their steps, treading a course around the bar and down the stairs, to enter the same small space where they had been only moments before. In my memory, I am recording these observations from the bathroom, as I sit on the toilet; I've retrieved this scene from my notes, from which I retrieve everything. In general, I hardly allow myself the pleasure of sitting down on a public toilet; today, however, I welcome the luxury of letting my cheeks graze the surface of the urban bowl whose convex surface had only recently provided a temporary home for my sidekick's ass. To linger here, like this, to attempt to adjoin or commingle another's body with my own, the past with the present, Marseilles with Paris, experience with transcription, production with reproduction, haptic gratification with virtual gluttony, is to name the unnameable, to assign a nonspecific identity to this person, this stranger, whom I have never seen again, a stranger—a companion—with whom I now share this text.

Verbal excess as the recovery of oral performance. Picture: a curvature that bodies my face, my lips and tongue, into a calisthenic mimicry or incantation. Drool forming at the edge of teeth.

Because I pretend a deadened intensity (at least in images), this memory, too, is interested in the aura of "spy" that, as a child, I imagined myself, or my alternate self, inhabiting, in the future, when I'd have grown up. This cool, detached demeanor lends its glacial mystery to several aspects of my daily life. I enjoy the eighties—the music, the films, the art, the tempo (a mood or vibe)—because I imagine the decade as a remarkable vector of deadened intensity. I was four years old in 1990. I was thirty-two years old when I came across my companion, near the Hôtel de Ville, in Marseilles. It should go without saying—have I already said it?—that when I travel, I like to travel alone. It's easier to be mistaken for a spy when you walk the waterfront, at night, alone, when you disembark the train alone, when you dine, ensconced in an alleyway and glance, intermittently, at the people nearby, drinking and eating and laughing and loving and learning and living, alone. All of us writing in our notebooks are spies, and what we look for is the secret rhythms of our daily life, found or created from within and without. If asked to *come clean* I would tell you—whoever it is who's found me here—I have no secrets.

Since my youth—I'm not sure when or at what age—I've harbored an infantile (involuntary, unjudgmental) admiration of the ass. In an earlier text, I'd written that in an earlier text, I've described these poetics as an aesthetics of ass play.** And what I meant was not only do I have a deep fascination, a deep desire for the buttocks, for what it holds and withholds, but that my writing, too, the act of composition, which has always involved an unregistered level of excess, of velocity, of a surrender that often feels like auto-asphyxiation, is akin to the recreational faculties of the ass: the verbal cheek or flab as ostentatious display, which allows—no, invites—a processual drilling, a foraging for hidden or nascent treasures.

Theodor Adorno discourages such phatic, basic pleasures as "culinary"—marked by an avowal of the body, by its surrender (to itself, to others). If I reject anything in this text, I want to reject Adorno's call to exclude "all culinary delights," where taste and smell converge in a flavor that signifies a sensual degradation. To surrender then, aimlessly, armlessly, which is to say unarmed but also handcuffed to a desire that actualizes escape.

Yesterday, the New York City Department of Health and Mental Hygiene endorsed glory holes as a strategy for safer sex. The three-page memo, available to the public, suggests that sexual encounters are best carried out in "larger, more open, and well-ventilated spaces."

** Maybe I imagined this book before I wrote that one.

Among the benefits of the three-layer, two-fabric washable masks include the masks' American size. Our Competitor offers Asian size while We made this to fit US at 5.3 inches height x 8.7 width.

To be in someone else's shoes then back to yours; then again to be someone else. What they miss when they return to a normal life is less the person they lost than the secret. The context, the atmosphere, the mysterious world where it occurred or did it. I heard somewhere that the closest thing to this undercover life is the experience of adultery.

Rough formulation for all things liberatory: we escape from taste to surrender to flavor.

Many Americans living in the United States were surprised in 2018 by allegations that a Russian woman, Maria Butina, had infiltrated the National Rifle Association and was having sex with well-placed men, in the hopes of receiving information for Russia.

For the four days that I inhabited what its website refers to as an "Estate King Room," the only program broadcast on the televisions of the Tarrytown House Estate on the Hudson were the quintet of movies about Jason Bourne, a spy, or perhaps more accurately, a CIA assassin.

Am I a well-placed man or merely an authorized person? Or am I neither?

When I was in junior high,[††] students were invited to participate in a project called "Operation Shadow." I'd remembered hearing about the project, I remembered hearing the name—*Operation Shadow*—because I had an older brother, and I had been waiting, counting the days, until I, too, would be allowed to undergo a training that sounded, in my clandestine-entranced adolescence, like spy games.

Taken aback, retrospectively, by the resemblance I allegedly have—never confirmed but oft-invoked—to Matt Damon. A taller, browner Matt Damon; Matt Damon with a mustache. In younger years I'd take this assertion of likeness as a compliment. In the present, meanwhile, I am alarmed by any supposed similarities between us. Do I still look like Matt Damon? Does Matt Damon still look like me? Upon hearing this notation (retold by me in the continuous present of composition), L says I only(?) resemble Matt Damon when I'm running across the Lower East Side at night, wearing black jeans and a black leather jacket—a feat I've performed once or twice—that I only resemble Matt Damon as the version of Jason Bourne immortalized in the five films that bear his name, the five films that have replayed in a row, every day, at least for the last four days.

Operation Shadow was actually an initiative meant to give students more "real-world" job experience. Each student, or group of students, was paired with a real-world professional, whom they

---

[††] Despite my affinity for interstitial experiences, I have an irrational(?) dislike for the term *middle school*.

would shadow *in the real world* for the duration of the school day. At around three o'clock, we would be returned in some fashion to school, to tell our classmates about the wonders of working life, to compare notes. No one else was assigned the group to which I'd been placed, a fact that made me only more excited about pursuing this game of shadows, entrusted to the role of sole apprentice, riding in the front seat and visiting homes—all of them empty— with a local realtor. I don't remember her name but I remember her magical keycard, an object (did it operate on batteries, or am I remembering this differently?) that granted access to all the empty homes of River Edge, a place that was already somewhat strange and arousing to me (my parents lived in nearby Oradell). Walking through the empty homes of other people, scanning the interiors for all belongings usual and unusual, was I learning how to become a spy? I don't remember responding to any of the realtor's questions. I don't remember asking any questions of my own. What did I learn of the real world, except that it exists to be subverted, or displaced?

In the Bourne movies, there is always a woman missing, or absent.
"Where is she?"
"She's not here, she's gone."
"Who is this?"
[long pause]
"It's Jason Bourne."

We kissed, naked, side by side, as sirens blared, and two men discussed something serious in English, marked by accents I can't name here, or won't.

At the swimming pool, another guest wants to know if L is Chinese. He paces above us, biting his bottom lip with his front teeth, asking L if she is from China. Asking if she knows how this started. You know, he says. Over here we are kinda immune to all this. We see all of this happening on the TV and when we turn it off, it goes away. As he says this, I wonder what's on his TV; I wonder if he gets the same channel, the same movie, or if he's watching something else. He stops, bends over, reaches his right arm to touch his left leg, scratches the scab on his ankle. He turns toward us again. We are both sitting below him, so we have to look up, if we intend to look, if we intend to look back.

I want to cultivate attention, but I also want to write absentmindedly. As I write this, Jason Bourne (the first?, the ultimatum?) invades my consciousness and thus this text.

I myself am provided with an ultimatum: to write with a tendency to forget, to absent myself, oblivious, unaware, emptied of all discernment, or to not write at all.

This is for real, Jason Bourne tells another man, in the bathroom or what resembles the bathroom, shrouded amongst white tiled walls. Do everything I say.

Everyone in each of the Bourne films is having situations, or relating them, over the phone. There is always a situation happening. We are looking forward to having others. When I was young or younger than I am now, the Situationists taught me that one could transform everyday life just by walking, just by redesigning the parabola of one's daily encounter with the city.

"Danger" arises through crisscrossing, cross-dressing. Following 9/11, a memo issued by the United States Department of Homeland Security warned that male terrorists "may dress as females in order to discourage scrutiny."

The ensuing operative strategy includes calculation (machine) and color-coding (security official): males are marked blue, females pink.

What is the difference between a defect and a defection, a defection and a revolt? The body as flaw or omission should be read instead as a sensual disavowal, an abandonment of the totalizing metrics of the state's biotechnological archives.

> here I am again, fixing myself
> in the gaze of the checkout
> CCTV

He looked up from the plate that had just been delivered to his side. She poured cream while her cup was being filled with coffee, as if she'd predicted the timing of the other's pour, or as if she would have drunk the cream-filled cup, regardless of the coffee that may or may not arrive, has arrived. You know as well as I do that decisions made in real time are never perfect.

Enjoy, she replied, your egg whites.

In the men's room—a place I like to hang out during compositions—at Broadway Bistro in Nyack, I am reminded that all employees must wash hands after using the toilet, before preparing food, and whenever they are soiled. Whenever they are soiled,

I repeat, thinking about the gift of recitation, of the difference between copying things out and speaking them. Outside the bathroom—several days from now—E will ask if poems disappear when you speak them? E is invited into this text as more than "character" but oracle, because E doesn't make any distinction between the sky and the ocean. For this reason, the reading series for which I've just recited a twenty-minute excerpt of this book (before it was a book) is called "Endless Blue."

Abdelmalek Sayad, who theorized the "double absence" of migration, also understood that the migrant, because they expose these contradictions, is always perceived as a threat to the legitimacy of the state and the conception—equally as arbitrary—of national cohesion.

Yet even more dangerous to the nation and its symbolic and corporeal governance is the second generation, the children of migrants, a group of persons whom Sayad calls "ersatz immigrants."

I want to read us as exactly ersatz: copies of originals who threaten the preservation of the nation and the reproduction of the national through a combination of defect and resemblance, a dissembling that unmasks categories of identity and conventions of belonging promised to our parents and simultaneously given and withheld by the public and its institutions.

I am fascinated by the blur that limns even as it alleges to obscure.

Today I spend thirty-seven minutes (an estimate) reading the "working titles" of other people's unpublished books, on Twitter.

One could write a poem about the potholes in Tarrytown, about their seismic alacrity, about the velocity with which I tear over them. A working title for this poem might be "Hole Fever," reminiscent of Jacques Derrida's *Archive Fever*, except in reverse; instead of collecting, the mania described herein would be an infatuation for abandonment—not to accumulate objects and knowledge, but to discard them; to be destroyed, to self-destruct.

Underneath this English there is another tongue gyrating against the cheek.

My wish to be suffocated by an ass—to be smothered, and yet to squirm deeper, as my only worthy energy—is my wish to resist trimming the so-called excess fat from this sonata.

On my last morning in Tarrytown, I had a revelation regarding potholes and a mode of composition to which I have often aspired. Rather than drive over—a need to conquer, to claim?—or attempt to maneuver around—distant, indifferent?—I would tend to my subject by driving under it, by hovering near it, or against it. Like a pothole, I would wish to feel the charge and shock of my subject, to sound out its weighty cavity, to be pulled under, to be dragged alongside its disheveled surface.

> another wish: for the writing to appear
> as casual, as flimsy
> as a snapshot

Nor to fill them (the holes, the subject) ex post facto, as if I were a construction worker or an artisanal confectioner.

Reminded of the story of migrant laborers, who, while constructing social housing complexes in Algeria and Morocco in the 1950s, would salvage, before leaving, the materials trashed at the building site to construct their own homes, replicas of state originals produced through reappropriation and renewal.

Around the corner, I pause to photograph a message written in purple chalk, leaning against a pole outside a shop's entrance.

THIS IS A

SIGN

YOU SHOULD BE

QUILTING

The sign communicates itself (this is a sign) but also expresses a wish (for you to quilt). This is a/sign/you should be/quilting, through enjambment, requires us to muddle the signifier and the signified, to renounce the communicative function of the subject altogether.

(+ an allure for "nonspecific demands")

At the doctor, to receive test results after having blood drawn a week earlier, I am met with a message I've received since my youth. "Unable to report due to significant platelet clumping." My blood, which I like to imagine as giddy, as joyful, as erratic, as carrying and getting carried away, is unreadable. Does excess return the gift of illegibility?

my insistent curiosity of texture, flavor, interior . . .
the makeup of things
empty, like
any good noun

Reminded, too, of an anecdote shared with me by a fellow researcher in Korea, who passed along an anecdote told to her in turn, about a Korean immigrant factory worker in the United States who, instead of giving his supervisor, line boss, or coworkers his birth or given name, provided them with the Korean word for "boss": 사장님 (sa-jang-nim). He never translated it for them. Whenever they called to him, whenever he was hailed, he would hear: "Hey, boss."

Several blocks north, another storefront sign, *masking for a friend*, solicits the drag of all identity. The identity that is the material conveyed but also the act of conveying; a condition akin to motion: to haul and be hauled, trailed, or extracted for some purpose, sometimes unaware.

When I began writing this text, my sense of flavor had evaporated. Nonplussed, I began diving my face into my armpits, my crotch, cartons of milk and cheese. Gliding my forefingers into the fold of flesh between asshole and scrotum. Scientists call it "olfactory training." I was retraining my brain how to register trace.

In another book, which I've yet to write, I encircle the aesthetics of potholes. A rimjob poetics, tongue in cheek.

W suggests that cheek is merely cheek. "Cheek," W writes, in an essay on celebrity, or their faces, "has no identity."

Does "loss"—every loss or lost object, memory, life—become heightened? Is "losing" necessary toward a desirable heightening?

In another book, W scans bodies for "erotic potential."

John Negroponte, former director of national intelligence, admitted in 2006 that the US was deploying about one hundred thousand spies around the world.

In this third movement, following closely behind W in the conga line, I wish to invite discomfort, and strive, within that discomfort, toward finding a "mode of home."

[remember:] the only delivery is non-delivery, a disclosure that is peripheral to the primary frame

This is what we call a stay-behind operation. So a country, he says, wiping his damp lips with a handkerchief he'd drawn from his breast pocket, places an operative or a series of operatives in its own territory, in case an enemy occupies that territory. These secret operatives, you see, are specially trained to let themselves be overrun by enemy forces. It must feel real good to just be dominated like that, don't you think? To allow yourself to be crushed—openly, enthusiastically, while cradling, all that time, a private desire. It must feel like heaven. Because in the event of occupation, you see, these stay-behind spies would serve as the vanguard of the resistance movement from enemy lines. Last licks, as they say.

When I lived in San Francisco, I lived like a spy, sleeping in a junior suite in a hotel on Post and Leavenworth for three and a half months, having just come in from London, where I'd been working for the winter. For three and a half months, whenever I walked through the revolving doors of the hotel on the corner of Post and Leavenworth, I worked as a spy, except I was gathering intelligence about myself, learning about who it was I was, or who it was I wanted to be in this life. For the rest of my life, or the rest of my summer.

Remember? At the height of the Cold War, NATO, the CIA, and the British Secret Service coordinated to create numberless stay-behind networks across Europe, Africa, and Latin America. Each network, he sighed, placing his palm on the crook of his leg as he leaned forward, recruited their agents from amongst the civilian population.

> isn't this film, I wonder, a stay-behind
> operation? aren't I, I echo
> the words written across the screen, a stay-behind spy?

Nostalgia for "signing on." A deep distrust of the always-there signal of presentation, the always-there signal of anticipation. A related question: When everything and everyone becomes available and prepared for, what becomes of fantasy?

(Most spies and potential spies lead a rather ordinary existence; they are not lavishly funded by their home governments.)

The line as anonymous duration, as a vessel toward non-identification, toward collective (and collected) meaning

Is all possessed individuation susceptible to individuation that is possessive?

Spillage (an industry term) happens whenever my balls spill out of their pouch during showroom fittings.

(Revolution as the improvisation of joy.)

In recent years, I type back, intelligence services have been hunting down the CIA's sources and, in some cases, turning them into double agents.

Remember J, years ago, "caught" and subsequently disciplined—was he fired, or only excoriated behind closed doors?—for "time fraud." Remember being entranced by this incident, by the ability (invitation?) to turn time fraudulent. A related question: What is the difference between time that is stolen and time that is given as gift?

Remember: what I'm after isn't filiation, it's alliance. It's combination and syndication. It's improvised dispersal. And memory—

In San Francisco, for one summer—for one summer in San Francisco, in a city where I could be a stranger and a stranger to myself—to embrace the collapse of identity as an everyday occurrence. Paradoxically, it became the summer where I could finally write about myself, to become a writer in *the first-person*. My task—an invitation—presented itself to me every morning, on streets I could and couldn't recognize, names that were not yet familiar to me—and all the faces, and all the faces. Not to begin to resemble everyone and everything I saw and felt. To resemble nothing.

When you receive this book, please make these changes.

I heard that people, like languages, were once thought to be impure the moment they began to mix as a combination. Unrecoverable origins, tainted by an/other's influence. An echo of the colonial—and extant—privileging of fair-skinned bodies, blanco and rubio over negro and moreno and mestizo and mulatto identities across the Americas, and beyond. I heard that the sense of distinction, in Pierre Bourdieu's summary, demands that certain things be brought together and others kept apart, part and parcel of the exclusion of all "misalliances and all unnatural unions."

And still I ask my students: Where are you in the stories you read, or watch, or listen to? And still I ask us all together:

What is a break, a cut? Or rather, what does the cut make possible? In music, repetition does not produce accumulation but perhaps its reverse: tonal and rhythmic improvisation. In that newly opened sound-space, we are brought to another beginning, which we have already heard, and differently. Maybe then, I ask aloud, this time standing behind a lectern during a symposium on diasporic poetics titled "Archipelago Dreaming," what I'm after is not the elaboration of an epistemic practice, or even a poetics, but a diasporic phenomenology, an unpolished examination of glide and caress, where the indeterminacy and ephemerality of touch— the immensity of minor things—calls into question the historical frames of periodization and essentialism, all those desires to locate, to contain, to grasp. The way every return begs difference, neither closure nor origin but linkage, a threading that should remain as "unnatural" as the overlaying of samples on an audio track.

So did he smack his lips or did he dab them with his handkerchief? And was it his palm on his knee or yours?

Originally, this book ended way earlier than this excursion—let's call it a romp—in Tarrytown. Was it fate, to reinsert these lines here, out of order, as I delay my own authorial exit, my own gratitude of "ending"—if not completion, then a desire to submit, to be submitted? To be in Tarrytown, a place I've never been until this week. To tarry is to be tardy, to linger in expectation—but of what? Jason Bourne's looming face, his small lips that look almost impish when reformatted in a non-widescreen configuration. Mine are thick, broad. I want to be cold, but I want to be warm, too, to alter the temperature of this text without thinking too long about why. I pretend to this deadened intensity so that I might beg it with effusion, with a love of verbal glut and the hunger to indulge. Recognition happens only when I look away.

what is a title page?

The crying out is the moment. It is exactly that cry at exactly that time of day, day of the week. As the body hits the water and the water hits the bodies beneath it, submerged or still skimming the surface of this great abyss, without which we'd be inconsolable. A body needs a hole, too. A hole needs the supplication of flesh, two palms, flattened and extended, and the head bowed, like this, under the laurel tree. Since the earth is patient. And all bodies land. Right? All of these unseen tears, this crying out and the prayer to abandon one's self. An infirm wish is still a wish. My hand above your hand above my thigh is still a reckoning. So any practice of notation is a practice of isolation, preservation, omission. Look again. What did you notice when you paused the frame and magnified the idle microphone, erect and unaware, in spite of its pining to be held? Rewatching Mitch McConnell inexplicably freezing during a press conference before being escorted away by stone-faced assistants.

I had been trying (again) to make a novel out of inessentials, the scrapings of others, an exhibit of things I've only experienced in memory, another for the things I don't remember, resisting the reflex to stretch the discontinuous and fragmentary into the ready-made logic of narrative and plot, to glaze my indiscriminate recordings with syntactic maquillage, in the hands of the sentence as it offers legible subjects and finite predicates. At what cost, I thought then, like I'm thinking now.

A related question or series of questions: In what ways does the selection of materials influence how and when and where we write? And upon what, in the end or at the very beginning, we write down; what we find when we become present with ourselves and for ourselves, when we allow the back of our minds to come forward?

This was the idea we had, because whenever I feel an awe in the back of my ribs, I try to return that moment of susceptibility to my students, who had been asked to join me in keeping a daily record of experience—neither a diary nor a journal; not an indexical attachment to daily life so much as a piecemeal investigation of one's inner world. Haven't you ever thought, I'd ask, just as writing allows us to think, to make a thought and to mind its erratic passage, so, too, might we retain the residue of the media that conditioned the act of writing? That what is produced by the writing act isn't only rhetoric or narrative, but the occasions from which thought arises. The landscapes and lineaments we might trace, with our forefinger, as if we were reading a map, or another book below this one. Rolling windows.

So we nourished the charge of discontinuous and amorphous encounters, the rapid shifts between imagination, observation, and sensation, learning to write by reading, which is to say by being in correspondence, by placing ourselves in another's orbit, annotating the flesh of the world as it continues to pass through us.

I think what we began to realize is that the problem of making art and the problem of naming too often intersect at the limits of recognition. And that what we were seeking was not an artwork so much as the surface flimsy enough to allow the traffic between autobiography, fiction, theory, dream, myth . . .

It is a kind of permission. To ask nothing of our accounting except that each notation could be the opening into another narrative: secondhand, secret, preliminary. Text as interface. Faces as fonts. Narratives as CVs, or anti-CVs. Backside and B-sides, bonus material, borderline traversal. Everything you could be doing if you weren't doing what you were doing right now. What if you wrote an entire narrative just by accumulating synopses? What if you wrote alternative synopses for stories that already exist? Or, I'd say: try writing captions for images that have none. Now wipe the image from your mind, I'd say, and render it from memory.

The way each detail recruits a primary image of its own once the whole is cut up and each strip of Kodachrome is magnified. Every character we've written assumes this urge: to escape the text for the scenery beyond it. But what is *outside the text*? When I remember something, and I make a note of it here, the memory too, assumes another life, a double life, neither substitute nor subordinate. I write so I can remember in reverse, which is to say, I write so I can allow myself to forget.

So my own writing had become a series of alternating A/V signals, dispersing like hyperlinks that do not cancel one another out but rather pile up, redirecting our gaze, like Benjamin's angel (belonging as much to Paul Klee, who painted it, as it did to Walter Benjamin, who, thoroughly infected by the forlorn eyes of the *Angelus Novus*, bought it in 1921) upon the trash heap of history;

dispersing like the flight, too, between proximity and approximation that feels so intrinsic to the operation of reading in order to
write; how translation, in its own way, nears by way of irremediable
distance.

So we recalibrate our rhythm to the impulses of desire between art
objects and their readers; the ways in which we are addressed and
altered by art and, moreover, the alterations we, too, impress upon
any artwork that offers itself to us. What is criticism but that sem-
inal residue, "generative," as another A/V writes, in a book called
We the Parasites, "outside the two-gendered model, outside the
matrimonial light of day way of reproducing people, wasps, figs, or
knowledge."

What we are talking about is the act of companionship, of making
a work present for one's self, without any degree of ownership—the
ekphrastic urge to show, and thus share, what cannot be seen; what
must be conjured in order to once again be considered. We learn to
be a parasite, as with any form of mimicry, only by looking, despite
or maybe because of the remove between the objects upon which
we cast our gaze and their makers' itches and etchings. The miracle
of reading is to turn this gaze into touch, touch into feeling—the
haptic glance that permits imaginative trespass: to put ourselves in
the whorls of the hand that writes.

The work of writing, the work of reading, happens then, not only
during moments of deep focus but especially of involuntary distraction; moments in which one's attention hooks to a single detail
of a painting or a film or a passage in a book, art that is now being
played back (but differently) in the viewer/reader's thoughts, to be

recast into something else. It's this "something else" that this mode of composing—whatever it is, whatever you'll name it—wants to index; the way a reader might learn to read the world through their study of art and not only the reverse, a practice that demands both an ethics of responsibility and the erotics of linguistic and identity slippage, vulnerability and surrender, penetration and discharge. The way that A.V. Marraccini, as she navigates the Centauromachy of Learning and Criticism, where the first lesson is that women are invited only for the parties, instead lays bare a novel proposal: the critical education of "mapping and re-mapping . . . the self onto the others of art."

What do we want, today of all days, but to be infected?—with the fantasy of a reading constructed purely by moments: moments of connection but also detour, moments of pathos, of impurity, of disgust and disagreement, of erotic encounters, of affective response more generally, a reading that demonstrates the indeterminant borders between theory and practice—as well as its ritual reproduction—of thinking and making, making and remarking upon.

The occasion for meeting, for convergence, takes time, and specifically, a time that is not ordered and uniform, that is not linear, that does not separate the *before* and the *after*, that does not repeat this violence (which is all separation) through monumentalization (which is history), a time that is not about closure but about the opening up of another narrative, neither public nor hidden, but nascent: the diffuse ways in which our lives are unfolding in relation to each other. I am looking for the moment a past becomes a post. Or rather, when *past* and *post* become part of the same transmission, belonging to the same space, the same breath, a moment to read and be read in all its dimensions—awaited and remembered and hallucinated and hypostatized—this thin paper surface as Möbius strip.

That there are gaps in correspondence is beside the point; the point, or one of them, is that reading, like translation, necessitates a poetics of contiguity, a *being around* a person or place or thing—a being around the text—that moves us closer to a heightened awareness of indeterminacy, an intimacy with the person and words with whom we gyrate, gathering tone, feel, mood—a frequency we couldn't otherwise receive, if, say, we were too close. Doesn't intimacy require this distance? Doesn't intimacy desire the missteps in our continuous play of approximate unveiling? The stripping of words, to get inside their coded information.

What does notebook consciousness accommodate? How does the decision to write in one's notebook inform what one will write, which is to say what one will find? A thinking, moreover, that can only be produced by writing, and a writing produced by movement, by mediation. That the act of notation shapes not only the past but the events to come—unintended futures—is worth re-marking upon; one's thinking changes even prior to inscription in light of the choice to notate thought. What we are talking about is a newfound sensitivity and receptivity to thinking and feeling in our bodies and to the spaces we traverse; the subjects and objects that move with(in) us. To acknowledge that narrative displaces the events it contains, resolving them as either "facts" or "fiction," is also to recognize that the notebook, as a second-hand relation, at once preparatory and unpremeditated, deters the allure of documentarian proof, the fetishization of unmediated experience that obscures the role of the materials we use to render thinking and feeling into words, words into meaning, meaning into materiality: not facts so much as diverse acts of composition.

It is no coincidence that Roland Barthes, in order to articulate another kind of reading, had to use the vocabularies of painting and the cinema. Since reading is an exercise that is nothing if not cerebral, bodily, dissoluble; the deceit of a good book is that no mediation ever occurs between one voice and another: the slippage of one experience *as* another's. A work of art exists for us so it may exist within us. Criticism implicates the reader in the collective "we" of art, which is to say the irreducible versions by which we re-member a single work of art in diverse moments. This is why every reading, which is to say, every writing, is conditional; this is why every act of love for a work of art is unconditional.

> moreover, I thought
> that by thus
> imagining the still fluid
>
> state of a work now far
> beyond being
> merely completed, I could
>
> share in the very life
> of that work, for a work
> dies by completion

"When a poem compels one to read it with passion," Denise Folliot writes, in the voice of Paul Valéry, "the reader feels she is *momentarily its author*, and *that is how she knows the poem is beautiful.*"

Valéry also understood the significance of approximation for the work of translation, the coarse murmuration—imaginary and nevertheless granular—that would allow us in some way to try walking in the tracks left by the author; and not to fashion one text upon another, but from the finished work back to the virtual moment of its formation, to the phase when the mind is in the same state as an orchestra whose instruments seem to waken, calling to each other and seeking harmony before beginning their concert. Translation as textual deconstruction, as synergetic performance. Can't writing, too, learn from this practice of reading? Valéry's retrospective meditations on the challenges and impulses of translating Virgil's *Eclogues* insists upon a fundamental decomposition: the desire—the necessity—to relocate to the *before beginning*, a retreat from crystallization to consider a text's preparatory coordinates. We return to an original, then, to understand not the thing made but the act of making. To distill the moment of origin, of formation, is also to seek out, and re-graft, the various and multiple conditions—both the other bodies of the orchestra and their instruments, but also the many moments of affective response between them—that would otherwise exceed the text.

How do I describe the quality of my mother's voice, for instance, if she were the one reading this (the one writing this), instead of me?

In 2021, Jennifer Croft, translator of Nobel Prize winner Olga Tokarczuk, said translators' names belong here & she was insisting on it. This clue, during the Double Jeopardy! round worth $800, stumped all three contestants in an episode of *Jeopardy!* that aired on Wednesday, November 23, 2022.

Behind every boomlatino writer—all of them, men: Juan Rulfo, Ernesto Sabato, Miguel Ángel Asturias, Alejo Carpentier, Gabriel García Márquez, Augusto Roa Bastos, Mario Vargas Llosa, Juan Jose Arreola, Juan Carlos Onetti, José María Arguedas, Carlos Fuentes, José Donoso, Julio Cortázar, José Lezama Lima, in order of their appearance, in the 2007 documentary *The Latin American Boom*; still others: Severo Sarduy, Guillermo Cabrera Infante, Manuel Puig, Reinaldo Arenas, as they are commonly included in more extensive surveys of boomlatino—is a woman, who has translated all of these men into English. The woman dangles, precarious, at the edge of visibility. Maybe the woman is effaced altogether, the way that every translation pretends a fictive conversion: from A to B, with nothing, no residue to mark the mediation of voices, the hieroglyphic propulsion of skin writhing as it is reset across a different body, and how the body changes, too, to accommodate the proportions of another grammatical code. The way that the majority of books translated into English are missing, not on the inside of their title page but across their front covers, the names of the people who wrote them.

The fifty-one-minute film, a part of the series "Fire & Ink: The Legacy of Latin American Literature," is prefaced by the warning: *Some language may be offensive.*

I wonder what could be more offensive than the omission of Ukrainian-born Brazilian novelist, essayist, and short story writer

Clarice Lispector, nimble interlocutor of the internal self and the outer world, who reminded Rio de Janeiro's public, in her serial crônicas: "writing too much and too often can contaminate the word." Lispector, who nevertheless resisted the prospect of silencing with an earnest affirmation of plurality—remember how, in Benjamin Moser's translation of her *A Hora da Estrela*, "All the world began with a yes." Remember the title page, in which Lispector cast twelve other names for the novel into being. Or Rosario Castellanos, born in Mexico City, raised in Chiapas, foremost voice of the feminist movement in postwar Mexico, whose poetry, essays, and novels share a similar concern: the violence wrought upon the Indigenous people of Mexico by a society still dominated by the norms, values, and behaviors of Europe. Castellanos, muddler of self and other, inside and outside, who understood that language was an inexhaustible garden, reality reducible to its signs. Or Silvina Inocencia Ocampo, primarily known as the wife of Adolfo Bioy Casares, despite receiving Argentina's National Poetry Prize in 1962. Ocampo, whose work, besides a selection of short stories and a novella cowritten with her husband, whose name characteristically appears first in library catalogs, was not translated into English—or any other language– until 2019, when Suzanne Jill Levine and Katie Lateef-Jan collaborated on Ocampo's debut, the 1937 novel *Viaje olvidado* (*Forgotten Journey*), and Levine and Jessica Powell worked together on Ocampo's posthumous novella, *La promesa* (*The Promise*). Or exophonic Argentine poet Alejandra Pizarnik, poet of the uncategorizable, the aphoristic, the anonymous, the impersonal, the secondhand, who would often first write in French before translating herself into her mother tongue, and who translated, during her itinerant Paris sojourn, several of France's most celebrated men into Spanish.

An alternate title to this combination could be called *Where are all the women in the scene?*

On International Translation Day in 2022, International Booker Prize recipient Jennifer Croft called on writers to ask their publishers to give translators cover credits, coining, in an open letter, the hashtag #TranslatorsOnTheCover.

Make a list of things that have been omitted. Make a list, I ask my students, of things that have been misplaced, things that were never documented, things you thought about but never wrote down.

I don't know what my dad's favorite flower is, or if my mom smiled when he asked her how he should say her name. What they each wore on their first date and was it comfortable; did they feel like themselves or did it take time, like my mother's accent, which gradually had begun to replace itself with another, to unpeel the veneer of the public self. Or who and what she desired before they met, what it was desire gave to her, besides herself, the knowledge of her body for herself. Or what song was playing in my dad's head when he boarded a small plane with a single propeller on Cubana de Aviación, with his sister and a single suitcase, to go to a country he'd never before been, so bedazzled was he by the rock music he'd heard on the radio that he didn't care—did he?—how long he'd be gone, or when he'd return to Oriente, if it wasn't a lifetime, if it wasn't a life. Or what my mom's first words were, in English, and whether she felt faint when she first walked down the Avenue of Americas, when she first saw a dozen people, two dozen people, three, traversing a single street. And that the windows had eyes, that the streets would light up, let you know when and where to direct your movements. And earlier, the discrepancy between sea and sky during the ten-day passage aboard the MS *Batory*; the name of the horse who brought them from their farm in a village too small for maps all the way to the coast, the metropolitan port of Gdynia; or what word came to the edge of her lips when she saw bananas and oranges for the first time. What word? Since none, at that moment, had been invented. I don't know when I entered the frame. Nor do I know what it feels like to be rocked to sleep, or to be held, for the first time, and for all time, as I take my first breath in this new life, in this new body. I don't remember my earlier form, or whether I was scared, as they say we all are, when I awoke again, with my new solitude and the freedom to reach out, whether I wished to expand myself or not; the sensation of plummeting, an unearned vertigo I've carried with me since.

What went in the one valise permitted? What stayed, which is to say: What was lost? I'd like to think that the valise remembers. I'd like to consult valise consciousness, remind myself that not all objects are subject to the either/or of acquisition and disposal. *Aren't there individuals who contain within themselves whole systems of individuals?* So objects, too, contain everything that exceeds their material dimensions.

How do our notebooks give us away, which is to say, how do they deliver us? How can our notebooks give us insight into how we read our past, how we remark upon our present? How can our notebooks allow us to access—and understand—the manifold experiences of a single event since reduced to the annals of fact and the formulations of narrative? To see is to know, a student once told me during our seminar on interpreting literary testimony. I asked the class to probe further. They'd been keeping their own logs—what we called our *records of experience*—for the past several weeks, and they were beginning to consider the ways in which their daily annotations were shaping how they interacted with the world, which had begun, in its own way, to imperceptibly alter, a newfound susceptibility nourished by the embodiment beneath inscription. To know is to experience, the student continued, without so much as a pause. To experience is to feel. To feel is to understand.

What I want to hold on to is where we left off; what we are left with. What I want to hold on to is feeling; what it feels like, a precursor to understanding but also imagination and displacement, the ingredients necessary for empathy. How the notebook, unlike documentarian reportage, is not so much concerned with what one did on any given day but rather what one was thinking; what, and who, one kept in their thoughts despite the material unsettlement of the present and the ceaseless destruction of the past, which is memory; what it feels like to be in the midst of thought, and how it feels to be inside another's. To know, in some interpretations, might be to experience, but so is, unquestionably, *to not know*. The desire—remember—is not an exact recording but an imperfect one: approximate, incomplete, annotated, transparent, fuzzy, fragmentary, discontinuous, remediated. Maybe the imperfections in such irregular accountings are the necessary cracks by which we might enter another's life and experience. What it might mean to place our hand here, too, and inscribe the words that would constitute this text.

what we are after, I remind
us, is the physical before
or underneath the copy / not the hand
writing but the hand
that writes

As I translate myself into Spanish, I find myself re-writing the English. The translation informs the original; the original accommodates itself to its translation. Before death and because of their dying, older bacteria will provide nutrients to surviving cells in the swarm. What has ever passed through me, I asked you, that has not already been mediated through another? I go gaga whenever I reenter Severo Sarduy because of Suzanne Jill Levine and Carol Maier's translations of his lush, pun-inflected, grafted Cuban Spanish, itself a translation from the formal Castilian of the Spanish peninsula. Manuel Puig, who taught me about the reversibility of high and low, original and translation, and about the indirect transmissions inherent in every message, was accessible only because of Levine, who traced his life and literature in the biography *Manuel Puig and the Spider Woman*, while translating almost all of Puig's major works into English, except for *El beso de la mujer araña*, which was written in Mexico while in exile, and remained banned in Puig's native Argentina until 1983, such that work on an English translation (*Kiss of the Spider Woman*) began *before* the novel's original publication in Spanish.

Maybe no other work has returned me to myself, but differently, than Guillermo Cabrera Infante's iterative *Tres tristes tigres*, a revolving tongue-in-cheek pastiche translated into English, once again, by Levine; Levine, whose corpus alone bolstered the export of boomlatino to the republic of letters' northern hemispheric metropolises, where Latin American literature could be properly codified and celebrated, where men could be made legible at the expense of women.

And to know it was not accumulation, it was not a gradual increase or my body's reconstitution and the improvement of strength and the articulation of tendons and ligaments compressing and stretching and my holistic advancement that would turn me into something greater but, on the contrary, my consistent discharge. An allegiance to form, for its disintegration. The removal and reorganization of my parts.

I wrote that in another book, but I could only write it because of Susan Sontag's introduction to Juan Rulfo's only novel, so hypnotic was her foreword to Rulfo's lean masterpiece, in which she introduced *Pedro Páramo* to Anglo audiences in Margaret Sayers Peden's translation by relating Rulfo's methodology: not to produce a book through accumulation, but by gradual amputation. What was left after each methodical erasure, I remember, became the spectral landscape of the protagonist's ancestral Comala.

The way that we understand these artists, their sensibilities and aesthetic strategies, whether boomlatino or the boys' club of the European avant-garde—nearly every written work of Dada and Surrealism we may have encountered in English was translated by Mary Ann Caws—is through a woman, who nevertheless has too often been orphaned to a title page. It was the wrong answer (the wrong question), and anyway, a man would end up winning again.

The shrouding of women in the field of translation informs the general obfuscation of the translated work as a translation, a promotional oversight that suggests a contradictory perspective: we value a work of art less once it has been passed through translation; we value a work of art more once it has been passed through translation—to the extent that the translation of an original adorns it with new life, but also, as Goethe foresaw, new literary value. Literary capital presupposes linguistic capital; this is why Glissant knew that the first thing exported by the conqueror was their language; this is why the prestige associated with particular languages has far-reaching effects outside of art: think of the theaters of politics, economics, and law, and the scholarship that sanctions public policy as institutional knowledge. Think of how the only thing more harmful than underrepresentation is the conditional representation offered by cultural elites and their servants (editors, publishers, agents, other writers), through which we become recognizable only by reproducing our absence. Harmful, since representation assumes progress while veiling the terms of visibility, which are nevertheless taken as the norm—to be imitated, championed, reenacted in other avenues of culture.

What I am after is not synthesis or union but the multiplication of differences, and I guess that's true whether or not we are still talking about writing, about reading. I know that as I developed as an instructor I developed as a writer, and as I learned more about performance and about everything that happens between the periodic flash of exposure, I learned ways in which I could make my writing operate as a rerecordable VHS—to confuse modes of meaning or pose alphabetical text as something else: a recipe, a haircut, a mixtape, an itinerary.

What did my students find through their annotative and iterative practice if not an ethics of care and attention that vexes ideas about ownership and generic constructions of genre and mode; the centering of copying, collection, and recollection as primary acts of expression? If our notebooks have provided my students with a moment of resistance, a moment of discovery, I hope it is the permission to write their lives into the texts that have *already been written*, knowing that every successive version produces a mutation to the existing order. Begin (again) in that unincorporated body.

With nothing else to write on today, I unfurled my left hand, using whatever ink, or a substitute for ink, I could find. Every day for seventeen days I would photograph my palm between the hours of 8 AM and 11 AM, and again, from noon until about five o'clock, because I sweat so much and so often, and since there was the real danger, as it was explained to me, of this text becoming purely temporary.

a brief layover
(cary grant with his
pants down)

During the credits, a green screen struck with blue grids dissolves into a city street, as seen from the reflection on glass windows from a skyscraper. As if to say: there is always something that leaks out of the virtual. As if to say: with time, everything that melts will melt, and everything melts.

(The series of names, splashed across the building's windows and presented in VistaVision, looks like an ad from the future.)

I once read that 75 percent of all movies set in New York City were actually filmed in LA. I am including myself here, my own life.

In the fifth grade I befriended a shy blond boy like me, who, like me, was born in Cornell Medical Center in Manhattan. We used to go down to s's basement when his parents weren't home and clear off the space, turn up the stereo. He had all the Billboard Top 25s from 1980 on. My favorite was 1985, because it was the year I was born. As if everything that ever exists exists at birth, or right after. We would turn up the music higher and dance. We were in the music video; the music video was inside us.

I like to think that all these chunks of language were just waiting, hanging around on my hard drive, my phone's storage, waiting for me to handle them, waiting to be assembled into another text, to enter into another life. All I have to do is look for them, to seek them out, which is to say: to remember things, to be reminded of what's already been written, what's already been felt.

At the auction, the auctioneer begins by asking: What's your pleasure? Then he says: How much to start?

It occurs to me that I haven't yet addressed the film from which this text's title comes.

The setting of *North by Northwest* shifts, without pause, without designation, from New York City to the California coast, Manhattan's Grand Central Station morphing into a car chase along the Pacific Ocean in the very next scene: north/west. Location, like time zones, is nothing if not tenuous, exchangeable. Here I am, dust ball of the middle of the country, waiting to be picked up on a dirt road surrounded by unsown crops and cornstalks, by a Greyhound bus, leaning near a sign that says INDIANA.

E explains the mix-ups as a matter of form. Erroneous directions: She says: Maybe I copied them down wrong.

All quotation is documentation, but also: All documentation is quotation. In a new light, surrounded by a different combination of words, sentences that have been retrieved so as to be reconceived, every voice harnesses a charge that is both artifactual and relational: permission to invite the past into the nascent awareness of its redeployment.

Aimé Césaire produces an "African" language in French. To be more specific, Césaire can *only* produce a language capable of communicating a collective heritage of Africa by employing the language of empire. To exceed the borders of the colonist, one may have to appropriate the colonizing language and the discourse of colonialism, to encode and reassemble, to return to the nation, if only to reinvent it.

If to copy out is to capture the trace of an earlier work and also to transform it, then the reader's marginal notes can be understood as a literal sub-text, a peripheral palimpsest, made possible only through the unseen interactions between persons, an inscribing that flattens the time and space between each actor in the text, which is not timeless so much as nascent and belated, dated, and also momentary. We read so as to re-read, and with each reading, we confront the text as an experience of emerging. And what emerges is the joy of creation to which readers can participate. No longer can we say authors ghost their readers, but readers, too, ghost the persons they are reading, which is to say the present ghosts the past by putting language itself in a state of emergence. Maybe the moment of spatial-temporal trespass is actually a reprise, in which every sampling of the before changes all the other records or recordings around it. The *be-for*, the after: in devotion to the latent interactivity of every text.

Unexpected time vs./& unaccounted time

What was I to do when—so certain of my imminent death—I had been given *extra life*? Some of us would take up poetry, or accounting. Others may decide to recite the five best strategies to secure a pasture companion, feigning ignorance about one's potential to wander. Recall the water buffalo who, half-eaten, dragged itself to safety when a pride of lions began to fight over its remains. Who among us hasn't been the water buffalo? Who among us hasn't been the lion?

So much beauty in showing the stutter of a source code when it duplicates, transfers, disperses across different media.

I am interested in limits the way I aspire toward edges; to lean in, bend down, make room for another or trespass zones that have been otherwise marked as "forbidden." This is what is at stake in any discussion of mobility.

Before Négritude, there was "pre-Négritude": an enthusiastic interest in African art among white male European painters. Negroes, Césaire says, had to be made fashionable in France by Picasso, Vlaminck, Braque . . . before the collective Black consciousness could come into focus.

Mr. Thornhill begins answering as Mr. Kaplan. R accepts identification as G, because everyone mistakes R for G, until R mistakes himself for G.

(What happens to R, where does R go, when G displaces him?)

"When a character moves off screen," André Bazin tells us, "we accept the fact she is out of sight, but she continues to exist in her own capacity at some other place in the décor which is hidden from us. There are no wings to the screen."

(For a single moment, over a dinner of trout on a moving train, G briefly becomes J.)

The idea behind the identity hijinks that characterize *North by Northwest*'s plot came from the curious case of Glyndwr Michael, a thirty-four-year-old homeless man who died in London after ingesting rat poisoning, and whose corpse, iced for over three months, was used as a decoy for a Major William Martin, a British officer who happened to be carrying secret documents suggesting plans of an Allied assault on Greece when he was gently pushed into the sea in 1943 to wash ashore in neutral Spain. No Allied assault on Greece was ever planned; no Major William Martin ever existed. Sicily was liberated that same summer, thanks to the British deception operation later known as Operation Mincemeat. The "mincemeat" in question, Glyndwr Michael, was not identified until 1996. In the fifty-three-year interval, Glyndwr Michael's body was buried in Huelva, Spain, with full military honors, as Major William Martin; the Allies won the Second World War; Berlin was divided into four zones representing the US American, British, French, and Soviet powers; the United States and the Soviet Union occupied a newly split Korea following the country's liberation from Japan; the United States helped overthrow an elected parliamentary government in Syria, which had delayed approving the Trans-Arabian Pipeline requested by US international businesses, the first of two dozen instances of US involvement in regime changes in over twenty countries during the postwar twentieth century; *North by Northwest* opened to a sell-out crowd at the United Artists Theater in Chicago; a bomb exploded in a parking garage of the World Trade Center in New York City, carving out a hundred-foot crater several stories deep and several more stories high, the first indication, according to unsealed documents from the US's Bureau of Diplomatic Security, that terrorism was evolving from a regional problem outside of the United States to a transnational phenomenon; and Cary Grant, real name Archie Leach, died, a year after I was born.

"It is," Cary Grant said, midway through shooting, "a terrible script. We've already done a third of the picture, and I still can't make head nor tail of it."

Sometime later, E asks G to meet her in Drawing Room E. A real room on the train or a self-reflexive invitation to extract another's essence, or to be inhaled? To meet me in my own compartment, to access my interior, at will.

"The car's waiting outside. You will walk between us . . . we will laugh in the car."

> At the airport, there are only two lines:
> Northwest
> &
> Orient Airlines

How do we organize if we do not have dignity?

Before articulation is exportation. Before redefinition is fetishization. Before I reclaimed myself, on my own terms, I needed to be seen as a curiosity, to be exoticized and eroticized. I want to remember to say that the opposite of the poetic isn't the prosaic but the stereotype, to the extent that it reminds us that absence is the first condition of all representation; that the challenge (our challenge?) is to assume every representation without being limited to it; without being limited by it.

After I turned thirty-seven, it occurred to me that almost half my life had been spent in front of a camera, working as an object or image and at the same time as a producer of words—objects, images—writing down the experience of dislocation, and fetishization, and commodification, which wasn't so unusual, after all, since long before I first found work as a model I found a life as a person who seemed to be born without a past, or at least a history that I could retrieve, and so I had already begun to practice sinking into the photo—disappearing—for as long as I can remember. It didn't occur to me until later, though, that in this world, many of us tend to conflate the inside and the outside; that to have a body and a face is acceptable and even sought-after, so long as the mouth cannot speak; that my image, too, like all images, would replace me, but not before I began to shelter myself in my own disguise, a form of mimicry and disidentification felt, I think, by any child of diaspora. The trick is not to forget that there is a camera here but to forget that this is you.

What is the difference between leaving at the same time and leaving together? What is the difference between not having a bed and not having a home, not having a future and not having a past?

In Havana, on December 7, 1969, Julio García Espinosa said that it is no longer a matter of replacing one school with another, one "ism" with another, poetry with anti-poetry, but of truly letting a thousand different flowers bloom. Art, he said, will not disappear into nothingness; it will disappear into everything.

(I was sweating and loved how the lighting was at this waterfall.)

Curiosity is a desire to know and an interest leading to a future in-quiry. A *curiosity* can also be one that arouses interest, especially for uncommon or exotic characteristics. Curiosity, from Latin *cūriōsus*: careful, inquisitive, from *cura*: help, care.

That it is neither impossible nor new to produce culture outside capital is worth repeating. Césaire speaks of the moment when he realized the precolonial cultures of Africa and Asia were not just ante-capitalist but also anti-capitalist. "They were communal societies," he writes, "never societies of the many for the few. . . . They were democratic societies, always. They were cooperative societies, fraternal societies. I make a systematic defense of the societies destroyed by imperialism. They were the fact, they did not pretend to be the idea . . . They kept hope intact."

It makes me feel like I'm living, sort of, M says, as he looks up from the collection of scripts laid out on the bed and directs his gaze to the viewer. Cuz it's kind of magical, you know?

The camera is like a giant tongue. (You can almost hear the slurping.)

Césaire's comments are informed by what was happening at the moment in which he was writing, as the question of what alternative forms of government to colonial rule could be imagined was being posed—and enacted—throughout French West Africa. Chief among these political actors was Césaire's longtime friend and collaborator, poet and former prisoner of war in Germany

Léopold Sédar Senghor, who understood that to address the conquest, exploitation, disparity, and subjection of empire, it was necessary to transform it into a pluralistic community, a community guided by integration and an integration that could hold, together, both equality and difference.

A common method of disconcerting codebreakers is to mix in with the legitimate message a message that cannot be decoded: a nonsignificant message, a mere assemblage of characters.

And anyway, if the text is to remain, shouldn't the text remain in flux? What would happen, for instance, if we were to include an excerpt from Kim Kardashian West's best-selling anthology of Instagram selfies? In the 512-page edition of *Selfish*, republished in 2016, we learn that photos are memories to me. As soon as I see an image, all of the details of the day or moment come alive . . .

In his 1969 essay, García Espinosa hypothesizes an "imperfect cinema," in which the evolution of technology would eventually create the conditions for the democratization of art production, or maybe, more specifically, unless I'm reading this wrong, the merging of spectatorship and filming.

If everyone made films, then life would become itself a movie, or rather: movies would become indistinguishable from life. When this happened, I began to inhabit my life, to attend to my life, with the same curiosity and awe as the viewer, who can only watch from afar, with one exception: I knew that the fantasy was no longer (would never again) be separated by a screen.

A way to frame both figures in the same shot, each one facing the other, is to position a mirror in the background. One person faces the viewer, their back turned to the reflected image of the person whom they are facing, who faces us.

(In this way, seeing and not seeing can coincide.)

"It's going to be a long night," I said. "And I don't particularly like the book I've started."

The text as decoy. But also as coy, showing reluctance to make a definite commitment; marked by artful playfulness.

It's in public where I crawl deeper within myself; in public where I can be most private, if privacy means solitude, concentration, boredom, and the insecurity I've always felt to be necessary for anyone who's ever pretended, who's ever felt the need to pretend in order to survive, in order to remake life into a series of indefinite coordinates, as tenuous as a sentence, the swerve of flesh on an electronic alphabet. Cadence of the sun at 1:17 PM to remind me I've lived this moment not once but twice.

In 1998, a plaque commemorating Glyndwr Michael's sacrifice was added to the war memorial in Aberbargoed, Wales. It reads: Y Dyn Na Fu Erioed.

The man who never was.

In a world of infinite reproduction and infinite reproducibility, the neoliberal extension of the market to all domains of experience, the commodity that remains most attractive (and most scarce) is not pleasure, but presence. But how to reproduce presence when souls remain tethered to bodies? The trick is not to reproduce presence but to manufacture absence.

(Managing one's own absenteeism is an arduous task.)

Despite playing him for over half the movie, R finds out G doesn't exist.

It is because there is no material source that simulation can arise, as both less and more of an impossible unreality. The point of simulation is not imitation; the point of simulation is radical transformation of the organism. Such is the paradoxical task: to alter one's internal being through external modification; not exactly to appear, but—like a powdered milk paint—to blend, to refuse calcification, to disappear within the variegated tapestry of self-bricolage, the entanglements of surface, skin, sediment; the innate animal desire to pass.

People also ask: Is North West Kim's real daughter?

"But I do desire the other for the other, whole and entire, man or woman," Cixous says, in the mouth of another, "because living means wanting everything that is, everything that lives, and wanting it alive."

Readers have asked why is it I can't write a straight autobiography. Why is it that we learn, the notes say, next to nothing about you by the time we've finished reading.

Rather than be "condemned to write only autobiographical works," filmmaker and theorist Trinh T. Minh-ha describes how migrant authors may choose to relate the details of their individual life while understanding that their account "no longer belongs to them as individuals." Instead of consenting to a subject-position that is "always politically marked (as 'colored' or as 'Third World')," in Minh-ha's words, or colored by ethnic, racial, national, or broader regional markers, I want to think of this text as both a renunciation and a renewal, wherein the refusal of identity—to be identified—in the *first-person* is a refusal to move from one form of dispossession (containment) to another (fetishization); to evade the circuit of differential supervision and supervised difference; to restore the origin story in the shape of an itinerary.

There is always something between us; sometimes a window is not an opening but a screen. Sometimes, no matter how hard we try to know another person, to know what makes them what they are, we cannot get beyond the surface that we are seen and shown, reduced indefinitely each time we think to look. Look again. Is it any different from the photo on this page? See how the picture of the printed picture steals some of the resolution, clarity, and detail; theft or depth of experience in every moment's fraught mediation. It happens again and again; it keeps happening—how the persons in the photograph look more and more like ghosts, more and more like themselves. I think often of those often invisible marks— trauma, shame, joy, fear, desire—and how these imprints of passage that come from within and without might tell a different story than the one reproduced in that limited grid of representation. How maybe a photograph is only ever undeveloped, but for the viewer to trespass these scenes of the past, and produce, with their own camera, another exposure.

> remember the book doesn't end
> in publication but begins here / here
> is the archive & the act of archiving

What comes first, the image or the imagination that conjures possibility into being? If it is not also true that in order to become what I am I've first had to copy out my life into words, to return the text to the body.

So Cary Grant, like the character he was playing, was supposed to be confused throughout the film's production. So Hitchcock was pleased, very pleased when his star actor exclaimed his frustration with the perplexing script that goes everywhere and nowhere, a story that wanders in a northwesterly direction.

The moment an archive turns from a site of excavation into a site of ex(-)citation (a site of construction) is the moment that time contracts: belatedness passes into becomingness. A related question: Can disturbing the origin provoke other points of departure? I am drawn to unbeginning as a possible scenario—a strategy of possibility—for everyday life. I return, and in the interval, I've removed the first three pages of this sequence.

(527 non-words, all of them tantalizing; I give thanks to be in the presence of that negative act; for sudden dispersal; to leave no leftovers.)

What is North (by North/West) but a repeating narrative of white supremacy and its deployment for political, economic, and cultural imperialism?

"We seek to dominate no other nation. We ask no territorial expansion. We oppose imperialism. We desire reduction in world armaments. . . . We believe in democracy; we believe in freedom; we believe in peace. We offer to every nation of the world the handclasp of the good neighbor. Let those who wish our friendship look us in the eye and take our hand."

On August 14, 1936, President Franklin D. Roosevelt addressed the nation in Chautauqua, New York, as Nazi Germany continued its methodical expansion and extermination across Europe. Nested within the rehearsal of democracy and fraternity, and the acknowledgment of "economic and political fanaticisms in which are intertwined race hatreds," was Roosevelt's framework for the US's own hegemonic program, what would eventually be called the Good Neighbor Policy. Among the companies that were to be sent across Latin America was Pan American-Grace Airways, Inc., whose advertising slogans—"Out of the Muck of the Mazatlán" and "The Good Neighbor Who Calls Every Day"—invited travelers "to follow in the intrepid footsteps of Pizzaro [sic]," in a "foreign vacation paradise, modern yet spangled with the glories of past centuries. . . . This is the adventure you've had coming your whole life." Tourists were asked to "play in lands" while exercising the Spanish conquistador's ambition to subjugate and annihilate in the name of Christ and nation: "Capture the city Pizarro couldn't!" In the years leading to the United States' involvement in World War II and extending past the Cold War, Latin America became more, or less, than a commodity but a set piece whose in-flight entertainment melted the divisions between leisure and imperialism, commercial glamour and geopolitics, historical reenactment and history's uninterrupted violence.

How do we know it's not a fake? R asks, no longer playing at playing G. R's outbursts cause an uproar at the auction. A woman beside R turns his way. She says: Well, one thing we know: you're no fake.

On another set, a father is faking his own death to "teach his family a lesson." The revenant husband, clad in T-shirt and jeans, will arrive at his own funeral in a helicopter.

[suggest:] a strategy for changing the meaning of texts (words, signs, media) through creating spaces where languages and cultures are not only related to each other but entangled: nothing gets replaced, only altered via the coexistence of presences, voices, stories

Any subset of a set considered without regard to order within the subset.

Toward an avant-garde that is not oriented toward Western metaphysics, an avant-garde that does not depend upon whiteness for meaning. If this is still less a book than a dance then maybe what I'm saying now or trying to say is that there is more than one way to dance.

Interested in our attempt to catch what Charles Mingus called "rotary perception," where you imagine a circle around the beat, and you play the notes anywhere *around* the beat.

I see that girl run on the street facing my house, F writes me, and I marvel at her. Today, I realized she runs on the backroad I take toward home. It was a thrill to see her run up close, and she gave thanks as she passed by because she knew I didn't want to be in her way or ruin her stride, and it meant so much to me that she said *thank you* because I would have understood if she had to control her breathing.

(I, too, love this *giving thanks* for breath, for pause, for [body] control—but only briefly—for breathing.)

The pulse is inside you; it is important only to remember the beat.

The first thing I remember about New York City is the smell, at least at a certain time: five-six-seven-eight . . . the smell of a city which was really the smell of people, of bodies, of bodies passing bodies, prickly and sharp, which was so much more profound, more haunting than anything I ever smelled in suburban New Jersey, where S and J moved, where everything seemed to have the same scent, where everything and everybody smelled alike.

I had written that the city felt as if it were an open road, a feeling I felt whenever we'd return, to visit I, my babcia, but it was more like a street corner, la esquina, a junction for pleasure, an edge for cruising or crossing, recursively.

Having never been to the West until I was much older—sequestered in an airport hotel in LA for a TV dating show—what, anyway, did I know about open roads?

When I was young, I didn't realize the effect of words, the effect of a single word. I didn't realize that every word and feeling was finding its own home within me.

(This sequence is 9 minutes and 45 seconds long, and it contains 133 editorial cuts.)

Those words, those feelings . . . I sometimes feel as if these words and feelings will be mine forever.

I like to say that B was my first translator, even though she's never translated anything I've written.

For a while, the only French I knew was: Je ne suis pas un personnage mais je me promène dans votre livre.

I never thought where I'd be, I never thought where life would take me, or how I'd make a living; how I'd make a life. When I was younger, I only knew that I wanted to try as many things as I could, pick them up, try them on. I only knew I wanted to reimagine everything. I never got bored of that. I would never get bored of that. I was the child of two exiles after all, two people who learned to live by imagining the possibilities of *something else*.

You could be anyone, I thought. Anyone, anyone.

I'm not a character but I'll amble about in your book.

Years ago, B tells me, I used to sit at home with my anneanne, translating episodes of the North American soap operas you appeared in. Before we'd ever met, B was converting me to A. My lines, or the lines that I'd been given, were returned, in Turkish.

For as long as I can remember I wanted to merge myself into the current of the city. It takes practice. It takes sacrifice, too. To become a mirror as vast as the crowd around me, reflecting every gesture with the flickering grace of an image when it moves and multiplies. If I could do that, I could do anything. But how could I do that without giving something else up? How could I do that without all the time losing myself?

I knew the lines; I knew the lines and I didn't know the lines or at least how to deliver them; I couldn't relate to them, I couldn't bear my own relation to the lines I was meant to deliver and had delivered and would deliver tomorrow and yet could not deliver.

(To write is to produce a video diary.)

Like Wim Wenders, who goes to Tokyo to pay homage to filmmaker Yasujirō Ozu and ends up creating a film out of his notes, his itinerary of images, his correspondence with the dead Japanese director, with whom he can only communicate in translation: by speaking with all the other persons involved in Ozu's films—videographers, actors, crew members.

In the film, Wenders doesn't use subtitles; during interviews, he narrates, in English, over his respondent's answers, in Japanese. The staging of "original" and "translation" melt. Who speaks? I like not knowing; the conflation of subjects, bodies, languages; the sonic beauty (discord) of hearing two voices at the same time, speaking slightly out of sync. I am interested in works of art that masquerade as reader's notebooks, because the most intimate thing I can ever know about you is what turns you on; what you've been thinking about, and with whom, and for how long, and how you got there (got here).

Someone once asked me how I feel about the oscillation of my own body across the written word and the visual image. Does it, M asked, invoke a sense of abjection or celebration?

M had been reading Roland Barthes's "The World of Wrestling" and the unspeakable heap was on each of our minds, whether it was flesh or something underneath it, like the vertical pressure solicited by a bowed head, the attraction of giving up all authority, if one were asked, if one had the choice. Maybe I'm remembering this wrong—what M said, what Barthes wrote. Maybe the transcription is buried, huddled in the same unspeakable heap that produced its discovery as an event, a thing that occurred or did it. Maybe I want *abjection* and *celebration* to be reciprocal and synonymous. People enjoy wrestling because they want to receive representations, to feed on images, not for lack of the real thing but to better taste it through absence and intensified presence. Maybe we need both.

In another version of this interview, I want to remain cloudy, indistinct, unintelligible, for fear that everything I say about anything

I've written will fix the words on the page, and it's less a desire not to explain my work than a fear of making the work explainable to me; I'd rather retain that lack of clarity that resembles the moment consciousness stopped for language, when I thought to write it down. Every transcription depends on timing, and here I also mean flow. I'm afraid of figuration. Maybe that's why I began working as a model. To destroy my representation through semiotic excess. The blur of repetition and dispersal.

And I knew enough to know that I would be created by the hands and the eyes—especially the eyes—of all the people I'd never meet. What I didn't know, what I could never guess, was that I would create them too, that they would turn to me and turn *in* me. And I would turn too. The worst thing was not that I did not belong but that I no longer belonged to myself. Imagine that. But I didn't have to imagine it anymore, any longer.

(Forgetting for a moment or just disbelieving—I was young then; I was unknown even to myself—that every pose begins as a trick and ends as a fact.)

S and J teach me English from an early age, because it was the same language that was forced upon them, forced in them, when they each arrived, across different bodies. It takes so much practice. And you may never get it right, the way that S asks me today what it is I mean when I read this back to her; the way I can't sometimes articulate a thought, when I'm asked to, in public. What it is I mean, what I am trying to say. What it sounds like; should sound like. It takes practice. And I know that practice means repetition, performance, mimicry; and I know that assimilation is my greatest pose.

What I wanted, more than I knew at that time—though I did not have the language through which to speak—was to take back control of my own image, my own body. My own subjectivity. I had first to learn to look at my body beyond the spectacle it served for others, which is to say to forget myself, or what I had become to the public.

Mimicry, remember, is never an exercise of exact repetition, never an act of unconditional homage. In the course of all communication there exists a gap, a discrepancy between what is said and what is heard. When the colonial discourse is imitated in this manner, it becomes itself rendered "hybrid"; thus, the colonized can subvert the terms of colonization by rehearsing it in their own voice, a moment where language, enunciation, and subjectivity become intertwined: to say what cannot be said; or rather: to make words say other than what they mean.

[i.e., language's oft-theorized constitutive indeterminacy is here on literal display]

Everything you don't see before the pose solidifies, to be degraded in gelatin, all the trying on and trying out, all the dips of movement in the face and the practiced tilt of a certain expression; everything but everything that repeats, I said again, silently, to myself, which means I repeated it too, I am repeating myself—everything that repeats becomes a fact.

Whenever I see a film, he told me, I dissolve myself in it, to such an extent that I reach the bottom. I fade out.

(And to make a trick of one's own is to solidify it within the body.)

The humming in the air was back to normal now. It was a comforting sound, like the heat of a radiator, or the faint buzzing of a mobile alert that reminds you where you are or where you couldn't be. Everything is safe and everything is in its own place and you are privy to every movement.

I remember sitting in the backseat, staring so intensely out the window at everything we passed, everything we were about to or would never; the outlines of other buildings rising from the background; the people inside them. Maybe not even seeing what I was looking so intensely at, the way it is now. Even then, I was writing. I did not know it, but I was.

Some dots, streaks, and black frames with numbers ran through the projector. Figures on the screen evaporated slowly, as though they were made of sugar and dissolving into water. A few uncut frames flicked by, scarred with dashes and white spots, and then there was another caption.

SHERIFF, LEND ME YOUR GUN. I WANT TO DO A LITTLE MISSIONARY WORK.

I stopped what I was doing as though frozen; it was as if the projector had jammed and left me fixed in that single frame, motionless.

"Oh, well a cut is nothing. One cut of film," Hitchcock says, "is like a piece of mosaic. To me, pure film, pure cinema is pieces of film assembled. Any individual piece is nothing. But a combination of them creates an idea."

What is the difference between a genocide and diplomacy, diplomacy and security, security and white supremacy? When Henry Kissinger died, I was sending this book over electronic mail. Not yet an "advanced reader copy," these passages still lived in the fraught dormitory of the cloud; I'd had to imagine them there, like any aggregate of charged particles, whenever I felt adrift, when I was sick and embittered, when I was tense and restless, the way I always am, the back of my head grazing my neck, my gaze at the ceiling or sky. The numbers are inconclusive, but even the most conservative estimates gauge that Kissinger coordinated the murder of over four million people—what some documents call "non-military personnel"—during the Cold War, over four million civilian casualties across the Caribbean and the Mediterranean, Asia, Africa, and Latin America for the purposes of articulating Western foreign policy.

In the movie, I'm kneeling in an Indiana cornfield but in reality, the iconic sequence was shot on California Highway 155, a spot of earth that hasn't changed much

[insert Google Maps image here] as you can see.

North by Northwest was a working title for the film, which was originally titled *In a Northwesterly Direction*, a name referring to the general path Cary Grant's character takes in the film.

It is only when everything stops that you begin to have that ominous fear: Nothing ever happened. Nothing ever happens.

Recurring nightmare: sooner or later, everyone is going to say the same thing, everyone is going to sound like everyone else (but he keeps hearing the words in his head, beating back, incessantly: *You were not there for the beginning. You will not be there for the end . . .*).

All day, every day, he worries about getting scratched from the script.

Right after R is shot, the scene dissolves to the sixty-foot faces of George Washington, Thomas Jefferson, Theodore Roosevelt, and Abraham Lincoln, carved in rock. Their busts shining in the afternoon sun. Cary Grant's body is carried out on a stretcher, into the trunk of a green Chevrolet—the United States of America above and below; what did those faces see, or oversee, but murder? The past as in the present, above and below, and in the middle, in the middle of the day.

A day ago, the President of the United States celebrated at the foot of Mount Rushmore with a fireworks display. He opened his speech by denouncing the protesters who have called for the nationwide removal of Confederate monuments and statues that have honored the countrymen who have supported and benefited from slavery. Demonstrators had blocked one of the major highways into Mount Rushmore hours before the event; many were protesting the Mount Rushmore monument itself, carved into a mountain called The Six Grandfathers (Thuŋkášila Šákpe) that is sacred to the Lakota and that, in 1877, was seized by the US government despite being recognized by the Treaty of Fort Laramie as Lakota territory nine years earlier. The United States broke up the protected land after gold was discovered in the Black Hills. During this confiscation, bounty hunters, buoyed by President Ulysses S. Grant, collected up to three hundred dollars for each Lakota tribe member they murdered.

Chevrolet's mantra, the year I was born, was:
The Heartbeat of America.

Mount Rushmore was constructed, according to its sculptor, with the intention of symbolizing "the triumph of modern society and democracy" that would radiate "a serenity, a nobility, a power that reflects the gods who inspired them and suggests the gods they have become."

Gutzon Borglum, who sculpted saints and apostles for the new Cathedral of St. John the Divine and the Metropolitan Museum of Art, was the son of Danish immigrants and a member of the Ku Klux Klan.

Today, Chevrolet's global ad campaign is:
Find New Roads.

What is the difference between discovery and theft, theft and the stealing of a people's history? And what what what

does it mean to pledge allegiance to a land that does not recognize your existence; to give thanks to that land that is not yours *as if it were your own*? What is the patriotic holiday but an attempt to humanize the settler colonial project, the endeavor to replace a history of brutality with the brutality of history?

Tu lucha es mi lucha—

several signs declared at a recent Black Lives Matter protest near the Arizona State Capitol. To fight racism is also to acknowledge how it has been normalized in our own minoritized communities, codified and celebrated as assimilation, as a path to equality, as an idealization of whiteness; to be *like* anyone else but me.

Remember the Congress for Cultural Freedom, front organization of the CIA, first convening in West Berlin in 1950, the day after North Korea invaded the South. The CCF, which eventually provided funds to the CME (Centro Mexicano de Escritores), a writing center that was founded by a US American novelist fond of writing about "tropical themes." The CME, which was launched by Margaret Shedd in 1950, thanks to the financial support of the Rockefeller Foundation, with the Pan-American aim of promoting "cooperation between nations." The MCC (Mexico City College), which housed Shedd's program and her idea that American influence could "make Mexican literature more universal in a way that would also deepen its Mexican character." Remember that in pursuit of those aspirations, Shedd exported not just US democratic values but the Iowa Writers' Workshop model to Mexico City; a representative classroom activity for her seminar on "Theme and Form" would begin with these questions for students:

"What do you feel when you see an elephant? What when you listen to hoofs? What when you see a horn?"

Remember that it isn't just language that the conqueror exports, but ideas; that smuggled in his language, as Glissant would later say, revising his earlier assessment, the first thing exported by the conqueror is the West's systems of thought, its systematic thought. Remember that in every pledge of allegiance is the confirmation of violence. That the alchemy of democratic capitalism does not just turn subjects into objects or persons into products but places into property and property into resources.

When asked to tabulate an obscure statistic, I replied: Four minutes and thirteen seconds of the film are spent showing Cary Grant with his pants down.

(To dream is to exist anonymously. Like a dream, there is an "I" here without any sense of self.)

Once told by an interviewer, "Everybody would like to be Cary Grant," Cary Grant replied, "So would I."

Like the internet, where everything is more true because everything feels more similar (more recognizable) and less familiar. *I have lived this before* becomes *I have seen this life before* and we believe it and we live in that fantasy, which is more real than fact.

In a redacted classified draft study of CIA involvement with anti-Communist groups in the Cold War, the Congress for Cultural Freedom is described as "one of the CIA's more daring and effective Cold War covert operations."

Effective, perhaps—but for whom? The CIA, whose strategy was to promote writers and artists of the "non-Communist left" to undermine Communism's appeal to intellectuals and prevent sympathies to Soviet morals?—or the writers and artists, many of whom were progressive agitators and anti-capitalists, all of whom were financed, in part, by the CIA, bête noire of the intellectual Left?

It was around that time that I stopped watching Alfred Hitchcock's film and began to remake *North by Northwest* by searching in the unassembled archives of my parents' past, my own sketchy present.

Unless the film I had been tasked with adapting had in turn engaged my body in its present state of modification, attuned to other frequencies and susceptible to dysfunction, subversion. The film, in a word, had entered me, the way a VHS slides into the black tape deck.

Since resemblance cannot be reduced to its manifestations in the flesh. Since to simulate is to pursue neither subject nor object—"woman," "accountant," "athlete," "soap bar"—but an idea. Since to simulate—isn't it?—is to proceed always from a representation, a copy, for which there is no original. This is why simulation is as much about excess as absence; this is why to simulate is not to reproduce but to subvert. What drives us to simulate, then, is not rapture so much as rupture: an attendance to holes, openings from which we might invite others to observe the alchemical oscillation between appearance and disappearance, which is all illusion. It's in public where I crawl deeper within myself; in public where I may be granted the conditions in which to simulate, *using the position of the observer, including them in my imposture.* If we require the gaze of another in order to better become who we are and what, moreover, we can never be, it is only because of the fiction of resemblance, a slippage between likeness and being that marks the effort *to make what is the same be what it is not.*

Among the different strategies that viruses employ to manipulate their hosts is mimicry; viruses imitate, in their adept athleticism, the three-dimensional shapes of their host's proteins to hijack the machinery of the body's cell growth, a ruse that aids the virus in their aspiration to complete a life cycle, which is death. Or better: disintegration.

When I was a child, and even later, I'd pretend to be doing anything else, anything other than watching how people moved, the way their upper lips trembled when they spoke or how their eyes darted when they looked up, when it was their turn to speak to the other people I was also watching, carefully, from a distance, thinking that if I could pick up on certain mannerisms, if I could imitate them, I would be closer to human, closer to having a public self, while retaining, trying to retain, my inner world, or better: to converge the world of the body and the world of the mind, to converge so as to not have to retreat anymore, so as to not have to withdraw all the time, even from myself.

And then I wonder, what does that make me? I wonder: what does that make me then?

And yet shame reverses any relationship of mastery. Shame, my shame, is what gratefully undoes me.

Dignity—karameh—became a rallying cry for self-representation among Syrian refugees in the spring of 2011. Dignidad became the birth of a new Chicano literary movement nine years later, spawning the hashtag #DignidadLiteraria to encourage conversation and engagement in the wake of the publication of *American Dirt* by Jeanine Cummins, a book critiqued, in large part, because of its lack of cultural literacy, including an inaccurate, voyeuristic, and sensationalized representation of border-crossers.[‡‡] What is dignity but the conditions to be counted—as human, as worthy of subjectivity—what is dignity but the permission to take back *control* of one's self?

Using Algeria's civil war of independence as one of many possible case studies, Frederick Cooper reminds us that "a total reversal of a colonial past can provide a rationale, if not a reason, for new forms of state oppression and violence."

What is the difference between being unseen and being unheard, being unheard and being ignored, being ignored and being forgotten, being forgotten and never having been acknowledged? In a note I've made public (What's on your mind? Hit *Post*), I remind myself that the work of representation so often has to be imagined before it can be concretized. I remind myself that Latino/a/x scholars are so often not visible in the academy—by the time I finished the coursework for my PhD, I encountered exactly no instructors

---

‡‡ Also: as a crass attempt to cash in on the border's humanitarian crisis, a point that was already evident, for instance, at the book's launch party, when publisher Flatiron Books embellished tables with floral centerpieces that resembled high walls, or tombstones, wrapped with barbed wire.

in the English department at the largest urban public university in the United States who hailed from the several countries of the Caribbean and Americas once colonized by the Spanish, Portuguese, and French empires—but also: we've been made invisible. Among all represented groups, we have the lowest undergraduate and graduate program enrollment.

A list of questions I have had prepared for each of my parents (to be interviewed separately) include:

> What did you miss most about your home when you left?
>
> What were your first impressions of the United States?
>
> What do you remember about language? About learning to speak [in a new language]?
>
> Did you notice a shift in your ability to communicate with family and friends back in Cuba/Poland; to feel a renewed sense of (dis)connection after 1980/1989 and the Mariel boatlift/fall of the Walls?
>
> Do you ever think about what your life would have become if you had stayed?

I have yet to ask these questions, to have this talk. I have yet to ask my parents to imagine *something else*.

Yet the structure of empire could become, Léopold Sédar Senghor and others insisted, the groundwork for another polity, not the congruence of nation and state but their dissolution as a nonhierarchical federation. The choice, then, for the organizer of angular resistance—signaling a shift, I think, from *anti-* to *de*colonial maneuver—moves beyond the conflation of independence as nationalism; it is to imagine alternatives to formal membership, to link one's independence with others, to respond to territorial politics and the independent nation-state by reassembling the governing code as self-reflexive and open-sourced. And yet the lesson, or one of them, of the same period of Cold War colonial decampment that anticipated the construction of the Berlin Wall, is that the dangers of a narrow nationalism are omnipresent, and even the most revolutionary political leaders, Senghor among them, are susceptible to its trappings: power, possession, nativity, the artificial sense of unity whereby a singular people should correspond to a single government.

The last question includes an addendum, in parentheses. Between brackets, I've written:

Describe what you see when you close your eyes.

Among the options offered by the laminated sheet stuck to the lobby entrance, through which I occasionally enter or exit, a laminated sheet that says HOW TO TOUCH YOUR FACE LESS, the one that appeals to me most is: *Touch a different body part.*

If we were to remake *North by Northwest*, stardom would be substituted for ensemble: Suzanne Césaire, and Olga Albizu, and Eduardo Galeano, and Tomás Gutiérrez Alea, and Julia de Burgos, and Teresa Burga, and Elizabeth Catlett, and Soleida Ríos, and Kamau Brathwaite, and Frankétienne, and Norval Morrisseau, and Pedro Pietri, and Yeni y Nan, and Lois Mailou Jones, and Lygia Clark, and Lygia Pape, and so many others, so many others, since

I've always thought the aspiration of any film wasn't to make a world but a life; and the most wonderful thing I've ever heard was a child's voice, and even more, what it was they said, having been asked what they wanted to be when they were finally grown up. I want to be a movie.

I have no gifts, no talents, nothing worth selling in the marketplace, nothing marketable. I am a sensitive person. I am very curious. I am indebted to the generosity of others, the generosity of my body, what it gives to me, what I hope to return as feeling. Acutely aware of my sensitivity for experiencing things. For being alive.

Notion of the "close second": *acknowledging the urge.*

Study the relationship between the event and its documentation, the documentation and its amplification in the archive.

I had entered (eaten, lived, etc.).

We grew up, Wenders told me, in a country that didn't exist anymore and was trying to reinvent itself. *We* meant Anselm Kiefer, the subject of Wenders's film that opened in New York City on December 8, 2023. What am I still doing here, writing this book? In the photograph produced by Film at Lincoln Center's media team and published four days later, you can see me staring, neck craned, chin pointed at a seventy-five-degree angle, eyes obscured by the 3-D glasses provided to guests upon entering the auditorium. In the photograph, or my notebook, I'm still there, placing my fingers to the screen while Wenders talks about how the movie needed a translator to pass the experience of viewing Anselm's art onto the audience, to make it appear before us, he explained, as an experience; how he, Wenders, had to conceive of himself as a translator and his film as a translation. I wonder if it was Germany that Wenders meant, or himself. That he, too, like any other exile, any other person internally displaced, has had to reinvent himself. And what did that mean for the movie we'd all paid to see, the movie that was shot seven times, and before each shoot, scrapped and recast. How maybe it isn't only Anselm Kiefer's art that speaks of time, Anselm's art that makes time, as Wenders understood, speak, but his own cinematic language; and then I wondered: How else could one represent this condition—homelessness, anonymity, exile—except for the medium of film, except for the careful use of archive and reenactment, except for their eventual melting? How I sat there, even after the movie had already ended, even after Wenders was brought on stage, absorbed in the small eternity of my notebook, even after everyone had already returned to themselves, aware of their bodies again with the lanterns lit, still clad or curtained in my 3-D glasses. Afraid, maybe, that if I'd removed them, the scene before me would have flattened into the daily death of unmediated experience.

Origin is such a tricky thing. I like not knowing where a thing derives. I like the typos and accidents; I like the emissions and omissions of our exchange. Like sputtering for breath or flesh. As if hunger was also your first language. To keep friction with no desire to polish. When I read this thread back I forget who is who, and when.

Reading *at a distance* articulates a suspended temporality between letters sent and received, read and returned. In the margins here,

I've written: How can I articulate exile within correspondence?

In another version of this story, all the memories of my parents' childhoods, of their unreturnable homes are in a few dozen rolls of film, which I never thought to develop until now.

I do not want to discard any of the identifications that are only partially available to me but use them with

and against each other to construct a concept for this kind of writing ("hybrid"? "migratory"? "diasporic"? "middle-distant"?), which would marry theory, process, and a kind of reading that begs nearness, that begs surface.

The temptation of pleasure is not to eat from the source but from the traversal, the passage from unknowable source to unknowable destination. Stochastic and intermittent yet gleaming. Identifiable in its edging toward awareness. We are led by and laden with this desire for traversal: not to be the other so much as to be the other side of the screen; to see and feel the bursts of intimacy as if one could be both sender and receiver, subject and object, host and guest; to be inhabited and to inhabit, which is to say to be both ghost and haunted.

Before I came to this text (before this text, like the virus, like any parasite, was within me), I was haunted, as all readers are, by the stories of others; by all the other stories we lived through, all the other stories we had had to turn into our lives. Bodies without ends, parts without centers. Memory of the one who listens, who is listening, as if I could gather, again, each passage, as if I could recast each exile onto interconnected videocassettes. Stories in which we could place ourselves, in absence of memory or the desire to forget, to have forgotten, where it was we came from, and the conditions in which we left. Sometimes I think that it was only the stories that helped us survive.

Blue flickers on again in a neighboring apartment, the cool metallic light of a camcorder that reassures us we are being recorded.

Outside this story, I would begin, I was beginning, years later, to track the movements of errant, personal accountings by migrants and displaced persons; the movements but also the moments, since it was my understanding that these notations were not just endeavors to remake space, but time. To enact a different temporal register ushered by the presence of the one who speaks.

Reminded of a conversation with W, months ago, when I admitted (confessed?) I wasn't sure if I was identifying a corpus of texts from which to put forth a theory or identifying a corpus of texts to substantiate the theory I'd already put forth. The difference between finding and forging has so often eluded me. Or maybe my point was that there is no difference. When I work in this way, the way I'm working now, the text seems to dictate words to me, as if I were the secretary tasked with noting the coincidental residue—to express the wish while at the same time producing the wish.

In a video chat, I arrive through description: a mannequin coat rack in the corner of my companion's room, and my delight to acknowledge its presence. As if the mannequin was positioned there, in the corner of my screen, just for me. And I thought about how the body works and how the body is worked upon; I thought about how often clothes stand in for the body and how often the body disappears by the fact of its adornment, and not the other way around. But to use a mannequin as a wardrobe reverses the alchemy: the body stands in for the clothes. Nudity is placed on display, except now it has another function: it also reveals itself; it augurs a revelation. Fabric hangs and droops and is borne by the solid body; it is the linen which becomes living tissue, capable of a kind of tension, the swift movement suggested by the outstretched hand. It is the body that reduces or retreats toward its own internal service: to camouflage, and to bear the marks of that protection.

I can only feel by hearing—

which is what it was, a thing prepared while doing other things: tapping one's toes, thumbing a thread through a loop that seemed to grow larger, more expansive, every time the needle returned, listening to something I couldn't hear (even from a foot away, sharing the same cool blue seat on the F) . . . it was Monday and it was Wednesday and I wondered when the changeover occurred or did it. I mean the hiccup of time. The way I pause sometimes, just to swallow. The hovering, warm air, which I can only feel by hearing. Which I can only hear above me. Despite or maybe because I've been listening for the music—the way fingers can dance too; the choreography of the body as its own ritual, repetitive gestures in view of the public. Right before each stop, a voice intones, as if on tour: This is—

But the screech and roar obscures the rest. Instead I'm forced or asked or invited to count each stop.

> I go on & go on
> the record
> I have neither
> the rapt habit nor
> the continuity
> required to complete
> a work of art
>
> I only have that tightness
> in my gullet, the bellyache of
> urge & blissful
> transparency
> a will to reveal
> nothing if not this
> migration toward impermanence

Where to? I want someone to ask me the moment I fling myself into a cab.

I don't know. Just keep going.

close, up

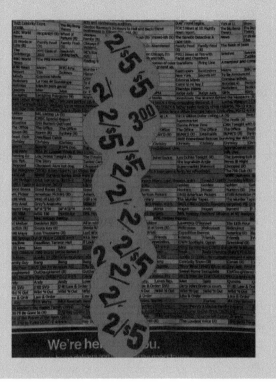

There's a story I like to tell, a story that was told to me when I was in Cannes, during the film festival, in 2011. I was there with a director, and a producer, and a few other people, whose names I can't recall or whose names remain unknown to me, all these years after. We were all of us using aliases anyway, reading (mostly) from a script that was delivered to us days before and then memorized (more or less) on separate flights. We'd all arrived in the Côte d'Azur unaccompanied, a day or two apart; I remember looking at the script again, for the last time, as I walked along the Croisette, trying to find my way to hotel such-and-such without having to ask for directions. In fact, I'd been asked to arrive tardy—and to look anxious, even uneasy, when I finally did arrive. The sun was out in its midday position and the breeze felt nice on my neck. I remember carrying the crystalline water, the rhythmic thumping of each vessel docked against the sand. I was meant to join a meeting already in progress: the director and the producer were having lunch, or maybe just a midday cocktail, with one of our film's aspiring financial backers—another face without a name: it was empty. The script, I mean, but now that I think about it, probably also the face. There were seventy-three unnumbered blank pages, which were preceded by a title. I flipped each sheet, as I'd mentioned, just to be sure, on the flight. And the whole reason I'd been flown to the French Riviera, from Buenos Aires, where I'd been shooting what they call a *lookbook* for a company that no longer existed (I mean today), was to give life to those pages, to portray the void or to reanimate it, and before all that, to find someone—anyone—at the festival who would buy it. I was not the only actor, but I was the only actor credited in the production. This made me think that we were already filming, and I wondered what I looked like when I didn't know where to look, or when to look, or how: the time and talent it takes to recompose the facial muscles, contract the eyes. One night—it was Day 3, I think, right before or right after Lars von Trier was forcibly escorted from the festival—we were on a boat; the boat was docked on the beach. There was a lot of noise, a lot of laughter, and some of it was real; I was afraid of almost everyone, afraid of their questions and their smiles and my own. There were several dozen introductions, and I was wearing pink—an outfit that had been picked out for me the morning I'd arrived, a day or two earlier, back on the Croisette. I remember the measurement, being measured, having to look inside that vibrating silence from so many angles. My shirt had been tucked in, a style of wearing or of being worn that I loathe; the full moon was almost orange, a titian orb. I remember looking there, at the moon, the whole time I was being told this story, which is part of the reason why I can't tell you who it was that had told it to me. *Who speaks?* A man, I'd been told, had passed himself off as a famous director because (as he'd told the judge) he had a great interest in the arts. The man, a printmaker, had never made any kind of movie before, but he had read a lot of screenplays. Soon after posing as the famous director—who, despite international acclaim, had a face that was, as they say, "locally unknown"—he befriends a family of cinephiles, promising each of them parts in his next film, and rehearsing each one for their role. All of the family members go gaga with their newfound proximity to fame, but also to art, the possibility of being burned or born again as an indefinite series of images. One afternoon, before the ruse is discovered, the famous director implores one of the sons—a twin, from what I gather—for a ride home. Specifically (according to court documents), he asks for *a lift*. While on the back of another man, the poor-printmaker-turned-famous-director begins talking about his process, and about filmmaking in general, and asks if the man (whose back he's on) has any questions. At some point, during the ride, the famous director tells the man, against the roar of the motorbike and the distant sounds of the city, that he's just gotten an interesting idea for a film. The film, which he'd lately been calling "The House of the Spider," is about two men on a motorcycle: one loses his wallet and has no other money on him. The famous director then tells the man that that very same thing had happened to him—it happens, he had said, that I have no money. The man rubs his back with the back of his palm, probably indicating the same stretch of flesh upon which the famous director had clasped, maybe even where the famous director had rested his head, from time to time, during the motivic excursion. Time slows through proximity to the subject; the mutual caress of skin and sensation; fame, art, the twinning of subject and object, body and double. The promise that that which has touched the artist's hand would now touch the viewer. Meanwhile, the man, with his other hand, reaches into his jeans pocket and starts counting out bills; the famous director tells him he needs more; he indicates the exact amount required to get home by drawing the man closer, whispering in the man's ear. When you're as close as that, I always think, I forget whose words are being mouthed, whose words are entering. And if not words, breath. And if not breath, what? After receiving the money, but before the two men part, the famous director tells him that the interesting idea he'd had for a film was like that: two men ride along on a motorcycle for half an hour. Because one has lost his money, the other lends him some, and they become good friends. I continued looking at the moon, long after the voice was muted, or the person who'd been telling me the story had walked away. What is the difference or is there any? I was there and I wasn't there. Not there if you weren't looking. I wanted to close my eyes, as if I were taking out my camera—a Canon PowerShot—to make a photo, if only to hold that orange moon there, to hold it up like that, to zoom in afterward, to bring it closer. I knew then why I had been brought here, why I had decided to come.

come to think of it, this time

I will say the words instead of writing them

Acknowledgments

Many of the images comprising this scrapbook were first imagined by friend and frequent collaborator Rockwell Harwood, whose ways of seeing continue to inform my work and, more specifically, the A/V signal of this book, the many modulations of which came at the cost (and gratitude) of my spasmodic nervous system, and the convergence insufficiency I've been ceded as a result.

Thanks to the team at WVU Press, especially Sarah Munroe, Than Saffel, Natalie Homer, Margy Avery, and Kristen Bettcher. Thanks to Rebecca Rider for your sensitive and perceptive copy edits and to Christine Hume and my anonymous referees for believing in this project and for shepherding it into the world in its present form. My resistance to house style's italicization of non-English words throughout this book is part and parcel of the book's desire to trouble lingual hierarchy and decenter Western logic. Thanks to Louis Daniel Botha, who captured my withdrawal for *north by north/west*'s final image. I also want to thank the editors, readers, and organizers of the following journals, edited volumes, anthologies, and symposiums where the sequences collected in this book, sometimes in different versions and in different languages, first appeared:

3:AM Magazine (April 6, 2020)
The Brooklyn Rail (July/August 2024)
The Brooklyn Rail (September 2023)
Diacritics 48, no. 4 (2020)
The Evergreen Review (Fall/Winter 2021)
Interações: Sociedade e as Novas Modernidades 34 (2018)

Revel 1 (Winter 2024)

Revel 2 (Summer 2024)

Social Identities 28, no. 5 (2022)

Social Text (May 18, 2022)

Zócalo Public Square (October 29, 2015)

Media in Transition 10: Democracy and Digital Media, Massachusetts Institute of Technology, May 18, 2019

Diasporic Poetics: Archipelago Dreaming, New York University, October 7, 2022

Thanks, as ever, to my parents, S and J, Zosia and Juan, Sophie and John, and to my partner, Lilly, and to all of my students and mentors who continue to enrich my thinking and writing—and to all of you, too, for the grace of reading and being read, for looking and listening.

About the Author

Chris Campanioni's work on migration and media theory has been awarded the Calder Prize for interdisciplinary research and a Mellon Foundation fellowship, and his writing has received the Pushcart Prize, the International Latino Book Award, and the Academy of American Poets College Prize. His essays, poetry, and fiction have been translated into Spanish and Portuguese and have found a home in several journals, edited collections, and anthologies, including *Latin American Literature Today* and *Best American Essays*. Campanioni's multimedia art has been exhibited at the New York Academy of Art, and the film adaptation of his poem "This body's long & I'm still loading" was in the official selection at the Canadian International Film Festival. He teaches creative writing and media studies at Pace University in New York City.